K—
QUICK

Judy Joo **with Jessica Do**

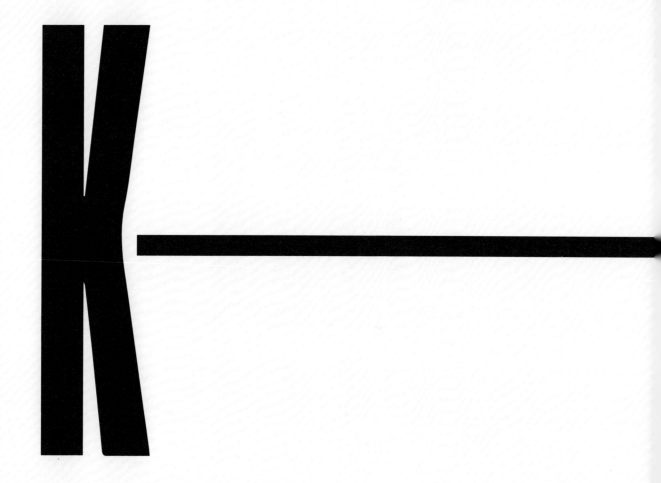

Korean Food in
30 Minutes or Less

QUICK

WHITE LION
PUBLISHING

Dedication

This book is lovingly dedicated to my mother, Chris Young Nim Joo, on the occasion of her 80th birthday.

Born in 1945 in Icheon, a quaint village southeast of Seoul renowned for its superior rice, peaches and ceramics, my mother grew up amidst the hardships of post-war Korea. Raised among six siblings during one of the country's most challenging eras, she vividly recalls attending school in makeshift tents only during the warmer months due to the harsh winters. Despite the adversities of the Korean War from 1950–53, she defied the odds, eventually pursuing higher education at Sogang University in Seoul, where she majored in chemistry.

Following her graduation in 1968, she embarked on a journey of academic pursuit, earning a scholarship for a master's degree at Ohio University in Athens, Ohio. At the age of 22, mere months after her graduation, she courageously boarded a plane to the United States, leaving behind the familiarity of her homeland.

Back then, foreign language teachers were scarce in Korea and my mom did not have a strong command of the English language. Adapting to life in America, therefore, proved challenging. She fondly remembers the novelty of being among the few Asians at her school, yet couldn't help but feel homesick, particularly for the flavours of Korean cuisine absent in her new surroundings. Biannual visits to her brother in New York City provided a comforting taste of home in the bustling enclave of Korea Town.

It was during one of these visits that she was introduced to Eui Don Joo, a classmate of her brother's from Seoul National Medical School. If you want to learn more about him, read the introduction to my previous book, *Korean Soul Food*. They were smitten, and married in 1970. Together, they settled in Grand Rapids, Michigan, where my sister, Sonya, was born before relocating to New Jersey, where I entered the world and grew up.

Thus, my mother's journey began – first as a full-time mom, then as a working mother. I recall her returning to the workforce when I was in fourth grade, obtaining her real-estate licence. Now, after over three decades in the industry, she has built a hugely successful business, and continues to thrive. At the age of 79 (at the time of penning these words), she is still having fun as a broker – enjoying her work tremendously, laughing a lot, meeting new and interesting people, and negotiating challenging deals. I think it keeps her young in every way.

Observing my mother's resilience and determination has been a source of undying inspiration to me. Despite the language barriers she faced, she fearlessly forged her path in a new country, challenging stereotypes and transcending limitations. My mom is a petite Korean woman, but filled with immense courage, strong integrity and epic grace. She is the epitome of strength and resilience. In Korea, we call it a 'fighting' spirit.

And, although she is busy with work, she's still an amazing cook! Her signature dish is japchae, but I love her kimchi and saengseon jeon (pan-fried fish) the best. She still makes delicious Korean meals for my dad, who is 85, which is why he is so healthy too. After all, food and feeding someone nutritious meals is a language of love.

It is with deep gratitude and admiration that I dedicate my third book to my extraordinary mother, who continues to inspire me every day. Without her unwavering guidance and unconditional love, I would not be the person I am today. I am profoundly fortunate to have been raised by such a compassionate and selfless mother, whose love knows no bounds.

With all my love,

Judy (the 'problem child')

CONTENTS —

Introduction

When initially approached to compile a cookbook brimming with recipes achievable in 30 minutes or less, I'll admit I wasn't exactly thrilled. I harboured doubts about whether I could genuinely convey my cooking and the essence of Korean cuisine and its flavours within such a time constraint.

However, as I delved into the project and conducted my research, I found the journey to be remarkably engaging and pleasantly challenging. I began pondering various shortcuts: How could I streamline cooking time? What innovative tricks and alternative methods could I employ? How could I simplify recipes without compromising on taste? And before I knew it, I was thoroughly enjoying brainstorming creative ways to whip up some of my favourite dishes in record time.

We experimented with hobak juk, a velvety Korean pumpkin porridge crafted from tinned pumpkin purée, and the results were delightful (see page 130). Our foray into assembling stews using pre-cut baby carrots, mini new potatoes and pearl onions – simply shaken straight from the bag into the pot – proved both easy and visually charming. Additionally, we discovered that packaged coleslaw mix, featuring shredded red and green cabbage, could effortlessly enhance dishes like tteokbokki and noodles, sparing us the hard labour of hand-cutting julienne strips. The list of ingenious tips, tricks and shortcuts seemed endless.

So, I invite you to savour this collection – a book that slashes cooking time without compromising on flavour. While I do recommend marinating meats for a longer duration whenever possible to elevate their taste, the majority of the dishes featured here are designed for swift execution.

Admittedly, some recipes may necessitate overnight chilling or brining, but rest assured, the active time spent in the kitchen remains predominantly within the 30-minute mark.

In today's fast-paced world, I understand that sparing hours slaving over a stove is a luxury few can afford. However, I fervently hope that amidst the hustle and bustle, people will still find joy in preparing homemade meals – and, hopefully, *K-Quick* ones!

Pantry

*Bae*_____Asian Pear
배

Asian pears, also called nashi or apple pears, are highly prized in Korea for their sweetness, aroma and versatility. With a crisp texture like pears, but round like apples, they're juicy and delicious. Renowned varieties from Naju can grow as large as melons. Whether eaten fresh, used in marinades, or added to kimchi, these pears are a favourite ingredient in Korean cuisine

*Baechu*_____Chinese Leaf (Napa Cabbage)
배추

Korean cabbage is the key ingredient in kimchi. It is known for its elongated shape in comparison to the rounder Western varieties of cabbage. Typically larger, these cabbages can weigh around 2kg (4½lbs) each and can be found in Korean supermarkets. Opt for crisp leaves, a firm head and unblemished white ribs when selecting. Before preparing, remove the tough outer leaves. If you cannot find the large Korean variety, Chinese leaf (Napa cabbage) is a great substitute and can be found in standard supermarkets.

*Buchim Garu*_____Korean Pancake Mix
부침가루

Buchim garu is a ready-made blend of flour and seasoning specifically crafted for making Korean savoury pancakes, known as jeon or buchimgae. Just add water and your choice of ingredients such as vegetables, seafood or meat to create flavourful and crispy pancakes. Or mix it, as most home cooks do with twigim garu (see page 16).

*Buchu*_____Chinese Chives
부추

Chinese chives, also known as garlic chives or Chinese leeks, are slender, flat and aromatic herbs widely used in Asian cuisine. Unlike common chives, Chinese chives have a distinctive garlic-like flavour with hints of onion. They are valued for their versatility and are used both raw and cooked in a variety of dishes such as stir-fries, kimchi, dumplings, pancakes and salads. With their delicate texture and pungent taste, Chinese chives add a burst of fresh flavour to any dish.

*Chamgireum*_____Roasted Sesame Oil
참기름

This deep amber-coloured, flavourful oil extracted from roasted sesame seeds has a nutty aroma and rich taste. Use it to cook with or as a fragrant finishing oil drizzled on dishes just before serving.

*Chamkkae*_____Sesame Seeds
참깨

Koreans use sesame seeds extensively, both black and white. White seeds are common and can be bought pre-roasted and crushed. If not, a quick toasting in a frying pan works. They're used in garnishes and dipping sauces for added crunch and flavour. Mixing whole and ground seeds together offers a contrast in texture and appearance.

*Chapssalgaru*_____Glutinous Rice Flour
찹쌀가루

Glutinous (sweet) rice flour is made by grinding glutinous rice. It offers a distinctively sticky and chewy texture compared to regular rice flour. Interestingly, despite its name, glutinous rice is gluten-free.

Dashida_____Beef, Chicken or Anchovy Stock Powder
다시다

Dashida powder is a savoury seasoning commonly used to make broths. Made from a blend of beef, chicken or anchovy extract, salt and other seasonings, it is akin to bouillon powder. You can also use it as a seasoning, to enhance the meaty or seafood flavour of dishes.

Dashima_____Dried Kelp
다시마

Dashima, or kombu, is dried kelp commonly paired with dried anchovies to make stock. The combination makes for a rich, flavourful, umami-filled broth tasting of the ocean. You will use this stock for everything, as you do with chicken stock in the west.

Doenjang_____Fermented Soya Bean Paste
된장

Doenjang, a dark brown paste with a rich flavour, is made from fermented soya beans and boasts a 2,000-year history. Coarser and more intense than Japanese miso, it's made by boiling dried yellow soya beans in salted water. These dehydrated beans are then formed into blocks, called meju, and then hung to dry and ferment using dried straw made from rice stalks. These stalks are rich in bacteria which helps initiate fermentation. After fermentation and further ageing in salted water for up to six months, the liquid is drained to produce soy sauce, while the remaining bean pulp becomes doenjang. This potent paste adds depth to soups, stews, marinades and dressings.

Dubu_____Tofu
두부

Tofu, a staple in Korean cuisine, is a versatile soy-based food. Made by curdling soya milk and pressing the resulting curds into blocks, tofu comes in various textures, from silken to extra-firm. With its mild flavour and ability to absorb other seasonings, tofu is widely used in both savoury and sweet dishes. Rich in protein, low in fat and packed full of essential nutrients, tofu is often mixed with meat, offering endless possibilities for delectable and plant-forward meals.

Galbi_____Short Ribs
갈비

Beef short ribs are essential for the renowned Korean barbecue. Whether sliced along the ribs in the LA style or thinly around the bone, this well-marbled cut offers tender and beefy meat. Blocks cut between the bones are ideal for stews, where the rich meat is cooked until it falls off the bones.

Gamja Jeonbun_____Potato Starch
감자 전분

Derived from potatoes, this fine, powdery flour is mostly used in Korean cooking to coat foods before deep- or pan-frying to provide a crispy and golden exterior. You can also use this starch as a thickening agent, much like cornflour (cornstarch).

Ganjang_____Soy Sauce
간장

Soy sauce, a staple condiment, is made from fermented soya beans. It adds a rich, savoury flavour to a variety of dishes, from marinades to dipping sauces. There are many kinds of soy sauce that vary in saltiness level and colour. For simplicity, however, I mostly use regular soy sauce in this book.

Gim_____Roasted Seaweed
김

Thin sheets of seaweed are brushed with oil, salted and roasted until crispy, resulting in a delicate texture and a rich, umami flavour. Packed with vitamins, minerals and antioxidants, gim is commonly enjoyed on its own as a snack, used as a wrap for rice rolls, or as a topping on soups and stews. It is similar to Japanese nori, which can be used as a substitute for gim.

Gim Jaban_____Seasoned Seaweed flakes
김자반

Gim jaban are crispy seasoned seaweed flakes that you can eat right out of the bag. These highly addictive 'seaweed sprinkles' are usually eaten as a topping for rice or noodles, and are commonly seasoned with salt, sugar, sesame seeds and sesame oil.

Gochu_____Korean Chillis
고추

Used fresh, dried or ground into flakes (gochugaru), Korean chillis are related to Thai chillis and lend a distinct flavour and warmth. These curved long chillis come in red or green varieties and can be medium to very hot in heat.

Gochugaru_____Korean Chilli Flakes
고추가루

This vibrant red chilli powder is integral to Korean cuisine. Made from dried and ground Korean red chilli peppers, it comes in different heat levels from mild to hot, and different grinds from fine to coarse. It harbours a slightly sweet and smoky flavour. Used in a variety of dishes such as kimchi, stews, marinades and sauces, it adds colour, spice and depth of flavour.

Gochujang_____Korean Chilli Paste
고추장

Gochujang, a vibrant red chilli paste, typically consists of Korean chilli flakes, fermented soya bean powder, glutinous (sweet) rice powder, salt and sometimes sweeteners such as barley malt, honey, syrup or sugar. Through fermentation, it develops a rich and complex flavour unique to Korean cuisine. Widely used in Korean cooking, it offers versatility – whether used as is or cooked. It adds spice and depth of flavour to a variety of dishes.

Goguma_____Korean Sweet Potato
고구마

Korean sweet potatoes have brown-reddish skins and a sweet creamy white flesh. They are sweeter and softer than other varieties, and appear longer and knobblier.

Gosari_____Bracken Fern
고사리

Gosari, known in English as bracken fern, is a type of edible fern eaten widely in Korea. Harvested during the spring, its young shoots are often blanched or stir-fried. Gosari offers a unique earthy flavour and a crisp texture, adding depth to soups, salads and side dishes. While valued for its taste and nutritional benefits, it's important to note that this fern should be properly cooked to neutralize potential toxins.

Gyeoja_____Korean Hot Mustard
겨자

Korean yellow mustard, akin to Colman's English mustard, packs a punch with its hot and spicy flavour. Available in tins (powdered) and in tubes, use this to spice up anything from naengmyeon noodles to vegetable dishes.

*Hondashi*_____Dashi Stock Powder
혼다시

Hondashi or dashi powder is a versatile seasoning used to add a rich umami flavour to dishes. The powder is made from dried bonito (tuna) flakes. It easily enhances, stews, sauces and marinades. With its savoury and slightly smoky aroma, a little sprinkle goes a long way.

*Kimchi*_____Fermented Vegetables
김치

Kimchi, a beloved staple of Korean cuisine, is a traditional fermented dish made from salted and seasoned vegetables (and some fruits, too), most commonly Chinese leaf (Napa cabbage) and Korean radishes. Seasonings typically include garlic, ginger, gochugaru (Korean chilli flakes), fish sauce and salted shrimp. The mixture undergoes a fermentation process, which not only preserves the vegetables, but also develops a complex flavour profile characterized by tanginess, funkiness and umami. Kimchi is enjoyed as a side dish with almost every meal and is also used as an ingredient in various dishes such as kimchi jjigae (kimchi stew), kimchi fried rice and kimchi pancakes. It is deeply ingrained in Korean culinary culture, representing tradition, flavour and the art of fermentation.

*Kkaennip*_____Perilla Leaves
깻잎

With a unique and punchy flavour profile resembling a blend of mint and basil, with a hint of liquorice, these fragrant leaves are often used as wraps for grilled meats, or as garnish in dishes. Their bright herbal taste and aroma adds freshness to many recipes. Although usually eaten raw, you can also pickle these leaves or make kimchi from them.

*Kkaesogeum*_____Sesame Seed Salt
깨소금

Also known as 'sesame salt', this condiment is made of roasted and ground sesame seeds mixed with salt. It is used often in seasoning everything from namul (vegetable dishes) to soups and stews. It is a much-loved staple in Korean cooking.

*Kongnamul*_____Soya Bean Sprouts
콩나물

Soya bean sprouts, found in soups and banchan, boast large, yellow, crunchy heads, thin whitish stems and long wiry roots. They offer a slightly sweet flavour and firm texture, remaining crisp even when cooked. These sprouts are essential in numerous soups and stews and are a favoured, nutritious banchan. Conversely, mung bean sprouts have smaller, less notable heads and thicker, more watery stems. They are also used in banchan, pancakes and salads.

*Maesil Cheong*_____Plum Extract
매실청

Maesil cheong, or plum extract, is a sweet and tangy condiment. Made from ripe green plums, sugar and sometimes spices, it boasts a fragrant, sweet, fruity, plummy flavour with a hint of sourness. Maesil cheong is added to everything from kimchi paste to marinades – anything that needs some aromatic sweetness. It can also be diluted with water to make a refreshing drink, or used in desserts.

*Maneul*_____Garlic
마늘

Garlic features heavily in Korean cooking. Its pungent flavour enhances the taste of numerous dishes from kimchi to Korean barbecue. It is a fundamental ingredient, contributing to the rich and savoury profiles of many traditional dishes.

Mirim_____Cooking Rice Wine
미림

Mirim or mirin, often referred to as a cooking wine, boasts a sweet taste and low alcohol content. Integral to many Korean recipes, it can be easily found in most supermarkets. Alternatively, lemon-lime-flavoured soda can be used as a substitute, if needed.

Mu_____Korean Radish
무

Korean radishes are rotund, dense and boast a light greenish hue on their bottom section. A stark contrast to their long, skinny, white counterpart, the daikon or mooli radish, Korean radishes are firmer and crispier as well. But, feel free to substitute daikon if you cannot find fat Korean radishes. They are often used in banchan, kimchi, soups and stews.

Myeolchi_____Dried Anchovies
멸치

Dried anchovies vary in size. Larger ones are best for broth after removing heads and innards. Smaller ones are made into banchan – either sweet or savoury, stir-fried with honey, soy sauce and other flavourings.

Samgyeopsal_____Pork Belly
삼겹살

Pork belly is a favourite ingredient in Korean cuisine, featuring in stir-fries, soups and barbecue dishes. Whether cut into slabs for bossam, or thinly sliced for stir-fries, its versatility shines. This fatty and flavourful 'three-layered meat' works well with kimchi and ginger.

Saenggang_____Ginger
생강

Ginger's unique zing and fragrance make it essential to Korean cooking. This knobbly root imparts a distinctive spicy and warm flavour. Whether grated, sliced or finely chopped, its aromatic essence elevates a wide array of Korean dishes, from savoury stews like kimchi jjigae to marinades for barbecue meats.

Saeu-Jeot_____Fermented Salted Shrimp
새우젓

These tiny salted shrimp are mainly used for kimchi but also for seasoning banchan, soups and stews. Use sparingly or rinse due to their saltiness. They add intense umami flavour to dishes.

Sikcho_____Vinegar
식초

Korean cuisine relies heavily on vinegars, particularly fruit vinegars, to provide a necessary tanginess that balances bold flavours. Apple vinegar (sagwa-sikcho) and rice vinegar (ssal-sikcho) are commonly used in cooking, while pomegranate, black raspberry and persimmon vinegars are popular choices for beverages.

Silgochu_____Dried Chilli Threads
실고추

These delicate, fiery strands resemble saffron but are longer and more wiry in appearance. Silgochu, made from thinly sliced chillis, offer a bold pop of colour as a garnish, while also adding a mild kick of heat.

*Ssal*_____Raw Rice 쌀

*Bap*_____Cooked Rice 밥

White short-grain rice reigns as the most cherished rice variety in Korea, prized for its plump, round grains that stick together when cooked, offering a satisfying texture. This rice is polished for a pearl-like appearance, but as a result is stripped of its natural nutrients. Symbolising wealth and prosperity, white rice was historically associated with nobility, while brown rice was more common among peasants. Korean rice is cooked simply with water, devoid of added flavourings. It is commonly blended with legumes or grains like amaranth, spelt, barley or oats, along with other rice varieties like black, red or brown, adding diversity in texture.

*Ssalgaru*_____Rice Flour
쌀가루

I often rely on rice flour to achieve crispiness in fried dishes, while also ensuring a gluten-free option when used alone. It's important to distinguish between rice flour and glutinous (sweet) rice flour, as they are not interchangeable. Western rice flours are different to Asian rice flours due to the type of rice used and the way that it is milled. For the recipes in this book, be sure to use Asian rice flour.

*Ssam*_____Wrappers
쌈

Ssam, which translates to 'wrapped', refers to a variety of ingredients used to encase small portions of meat or other fillings. While the most common wrappings include leafy greens like red oak lettuce or perilla leaves (kkaennip), ssam can also feature thinly sliced radish (mu ssam), kimchi (kimchi ssam), roasted seaweed (gim ssam) and more. I'll often say, 'serve with ssam' in this book, which means offer the dish with some leaves to wrap up bites of the main dish.

*Tteok*_____Rice Cakes
떡

These chewy, dense rice cakes come in various shapes, sizes and widths, and are made from glutinous (sweet) rice flour. They're versatile, enjoyed in soups, stir-fries or simply toasted. With their toothsome texture, they're a childhood favourite. Typically served on New Year's Day, they're used in both sweet and savoury dishes. Sold as cylindrical sticks (garae-tteok), sliced into oval-shaped discs (tteokgukyong-tteok) or moulded into mini hearts, balls, stars and moons (joraengi-tteok), they add a satisfying bite to any dish.

*Twigim Garu*_____Korean Frying Mix
튀김가루

Twigim garu, also known as frying mix, is a packaged specialized blend of flour and seasonings designed specifically for making Korean-style fried foods, known as twigim. Similar to tempura batter, this ready-to-use mix is a staple in most households. Just add water and dip your desired ingredients in the batter, then fry until golden brown for deliciously crispy results.

*Yujacha*_____Citron Tea Syrup
유자차

Sold in glass jars, this marmalade-like citron honey, is commonly used for brewing tea. Made from yuja, or yuzu in Japanese, it imparts a fragrant and floral citrus flavour, reminiscent of a blend of lemon and tangerine. Besides tea, I incorporate it into various desserts and sweet snacks.

BANCHAN & CO

SMALL PLATES

가지나물

SERVES 4

Prep time: 12 minutes
Total time: 20 minutes

450g (1lb) Japanese or Korean
 aubergines (eggplants)
2 tbsp soy sauce, plus extra
 as needed
½ tsp mirim
2 spring onions (scallions), thinly
 sliced
1 tsp grated garlic
1 tsp kkaesogeum (sesame seed salt)
2 tsp roasted sesame oil
½ tsp gochugaru (Korean chilli flakes)
freshly ground black pepper
sea or kosher salt

To Serve
sprinkle of black sesame seeds
sprinkle of roasted sesame seeds
½ spring onion (scallion), thinly sliced

Aubergine Banchan

Gaji Namul

Banchan means 'side dish' in Korean and refers to the many small plates that are served with every meal. These dishes can be varieties of kimchi, vegetables (namul), fish, meat and more. They can be served in many different ways including raw (salads), braised (jorim), pan-fried (jeon), fermented and pickled. The most popular banchan are usually namul dishes with spinach, bean sprouts, aubergine (eggplant) and beans being some of the most loved.

This easy side dish never fails to impress a crowd. Feel free to serve it warm or cold and use any kind of aubergines you can find, although the thin, long Japanese/Korean varieties work best.

Trim the aubergines and cut them into quarters lengthwise, then into thirds crosswise (about 5–6cm/2–2½in long pieces).

Place a steamer basket in the bottom of a large saucepan, and fill with enough water to just reach the bottom of the basket. Place the aubergines in the basket, spreading them around evenly, then place the pan over a high heat and cover. Steam the aubergines for 7–8 minutes until soft. Remove from the heat and allow to cool until comfortable to handle.

Alternatively, using a fork, poke holes all over the aubergines and place in a large, heatproof bowl. Cover the bowl with a heatproof plate and microwave until tender, about 7 minutes. Remove from the microwave, uncover and set aside to cool.

Meanwhile, in a medium bowl, whisk together the soy sauce, mirim, spring onions, garlic, kkaesogeum, sesame oil, gochugaru and pepper to taste.

Place the cooled aubergines on a cutting board and slice lengthwise into 1cm (½in) thick batons. Place the strips into the soy sauce mixture and toss carefully to coat. Season with more soy sauce or salt to taste. Garnish with sesame seeds and spring onions to serve.

콩나물무침

Soya Bean Sprout Banchan

Kongnamul Muchim

SERVES 4

Prep time: 10 minutes
Total time: 20 minutes

340g (12oz) soya bean sprouts (tails
   and any brown pieces removed)
1 spring onion (scallion), thinly sliced
1 garlic clove, grated
1 tbsp roasted sesame seeds
1 tsp gochugaru (Korean chilli flakes)
1 tbsp roasted sesame oil
sea or kosher salt

These sprouts, boasting vibrant, crunchy yellow heads, hold a special place as my family's favourite banchan. I fondly recall sitting with my mom and grandmother, meticulously removing the wiry roots while engrossed in Korean dramas. It is not necessary to pick off the roots, as it is time consuming, but it does make for a more attractive finish. This dish is the ideal accompaniment to Bountiful Bibimbap (see page 135) or Folded Kimbap (see page 122), adding delightful crunch and flavour.

Rinse the sprouts well, then quickly pick through the sprouts, discarding any loose husks, brown heads and loose roots.

In a medium saucepan, combine the sprouts, 120ml (½ cup) water and a generous pinch of salt. Cover, bring to the boil over a high heat and boil for about 10 minutes. Drain, rinse under cold water until cool, and drain again well. Gently squeeze out any excess water.

In a medium bowl, stir together the spring onion, garlic, sesame seeds, gochugaru and sesame oil. Add the bean sprouts, season with salt to taste and toss to coat.

Serve immediately or place in the fridge and serve chilled.

시금치나물

Spinach Banchan

Sigeumchi Namul

SERVES 4

_____

Prep time: 10 minutes
Total time: 15 minutes

1 tbsp vegetable or other neutral oil
450g (1lb) spinach, stems trimmed
2 tbsp roasted sesame oil
1 tbsp soy sauce
1 tsp roasted sesame seeds, crushed
2 garlic cloves, grated
1 spring onion (scallion), trimmed and
  thinly sliced
sea or kosher salt
freshly ground black pepper

This straightforward spinach side dish is a staple at both restaurants and home tables alike. It's versatile enough to be used in Bountiful Bibimbap (see page 135) or in Folded Kimbap (see page 122). While blanching the spinach in boiling water and squeezing out excess moisture is a more traditional method, sautéing offers a quicker alternative.

Heat a large non-stick frying pan over a medium-high heat. Add the oil and all the spinach. Sauté for 4–5 minutes until the spinach is wilted. Put the cooked spinach in a colander or sieve and press with a wooden spoon or non-stick spatula to squeeze out the excess liquid.

In a medium bowl, whisk together the sesame oil, soy sauce, sesame seeds, garlic, spring onion, salt and pepper to taste. Add the spinach and then toss together, mixing well. Serve immediately or chill in the fridge, then serve.

무나물

Radish Banchan

Mu Namul

SERVES 4–6

Prep time: 16 minutes
Total time: 20 minutes

450g (1lb) mu (Korean radish)
vegetable or other neutral oil,
  for cooking
1 large garlic clove, grated
2 tsp fish sauce or light soy sauce
2 tbsp Anchovy Dashi Stock (see
  page 192) or Vegetarian Dashi
  Stock (see page 193) or water
2 spring onions (scallions), thinly
  sliced, both white and green parts
1 tbsp roasted sesame oil
1 tsp roasted sesame seeds
sea or kosher salt

<u>To Serve</u>
roasted sesame seeds
½ spring onion (scallion), thinly sliced

Mu, or Korean radish, is in season in the autumn (fall) and winter, but is available all year round. When in season, this white and green radish is sweet and fragrant. Out of season, it tends to be a bit more bitter. Adjust the seasoning accordingly and even add a pinch of sugar to offset any harsh notes. Feel free to make the dashi stock from dashida powder or bouillon; it will boost the flavour of this well-loved side dish. It is best to let this banchan sit and pickle for at least a few hours or overnight, but it can also be enjoyed right away.

Trim and peel the radish. Cut the radish into matchsticks about 5 x 5mm (⅛ x ⅛in wide).

Place a large non-stick frying pan over a medium heat and drizzle with vegetable oil. Add the garlic and radish and sauté for about 1 minute, then add the fish sauce or soy sauce. Add the stock or water and cover with a lid. Turn up to a medium-high heat and cook for about 3 minutes until softened but still slightly firm, stirring occasionally to ensure even cooking. Place the cooked radish in a bowl and gently mix in the spring onions, sesame oil, sesame seeds and salt to taste.

To finish, sprinkle over more sesame seeds and spring onions, then serve warm or at room temperature.

<u>Tip</u>
Feel free to use daikon or mouli, if you cannot find Korean radishes.

계란찜

SERVES 2–4

Prep time: 5 minutes
Total time: 15 minutes

4 large eggs (about 225g/8oz)
1 tsp fish sauce or saeu-jeot
  (salted shrimp)
¼ tsp sea or kosher salt
2 spring onions (scallions), thinly
  sliced, plus extra to serve
115ml (½ cup) chicken stock
freshly ground black pepper

To Serve
drizzle of roasted sesame oil
sprinkling of roasted sesame seeds

Comforting Egg Custard Soufflé

Gyeranjjim

My little friend, Leah, loves this fluffy egg so much that I had to teach her mom, Annie, how to make it. It's so easy that now she will regularly whip this up as an afterschool snack with rice.

It's important to use the correct sized pot to prevent overflow as the soufflé rises; too small a pot can lead to spillage, while too large a pot may result in less doming. Nonetheless, the flavour will still be excellent. Feel free to substitute instant or homemade dashi stock for chicken stock as you like. For a vegetarian version, use veggie dashi stock and replace the fish sauce with light soy sauce, though note that the custard's colour may be slightly darker.

In a medium bowl, whisk together the eggs, then add the fish sauce, salt, pepper to taste and the spring onions. Set aside.

Pour the chicken stock into a ttukbaegi ceramic pot (500ml/½ quart size) or similar-sized saucepan and set on the stove over a high heat. Bring the stock to the boil, about 4 minutes.

Reduce the heat to medium and slowly pour in the egg mixture, stirring gently with a spoon or small non-stick spatula to form curds, about 3 minutes. The egg mixture should look almost cooked through.

Reduce the heat to low and cover the pot with an upside-down heatproof bowl to create a dome over the top, and allow to steam for 2–3 minutes. Turn off the heat and, using oven mitts or a thick dish cloth, carefully remove the bowl from the pot. The eggs should have risen and look fluffy.

Top the souffle with the spring onions, a drizzle of sesame oil and a sprinkle of sesame seeds. Serve immediately.

양념두부 튀김

SERVES 1–2

Prep time: 16 minutes
Total time: 30 minutes

400g (14oz) block of extra-firm tofu, drained
1 tbsp soy sauce, plus extra as needed
2 tbsp light brown sugar, plus extra as needed
½ tbsp gochujang (Korean chilli paste)
1 tsp rice vinegar
½ tsp roasted sesame oil
2 garlic cloves, grated
1 tsp grated ginger
1 tbsp cornflour (cornstarch), plus 60g (½ cup) for dredging
60ml (¼ cup) vegetable or other neutral oil

To Serve

micro Chinese chives or purple shiso

Crispy Tofu with Barbecue Sauce

Yangnyeom Dubu Twigim

For optimal results, choose firm or extra-firm tofu to achieve the best texture. You'll relish the irresistible combination of this sweet and spicy barbecue sauce too, resulting in a crispy and utterly addictive bite. Feel free to make extra sauce and use it to drizzle on top of other vegetables or proteins.

Cut the tofu into four even pieces, then slice each piece in half. Place on a plate lined with paper towels. You should have eight square pieces. Set aside.

In a small saucepan, whisk together the soy sauce, sugar, gochujang, vinegar, sesame oil, garlic and ginger. Place over a medium heat and bring to a low simmer, mixing well.

In a small bowl, whisk the cornflour with 60ml (¼ cup) water and then mix into the sauce. Simmer until thickened (about 1 minute), then remove from the heat. Taste and adjust the seasoning, adding more sugar or soy sauce as needed. Set aside.

Pour the remaining cornflour into a shallow bowl and dredge the tofu slices, shaking off any excess, then lay the tofu on a wire rack placed over a tray.

Place a large non-stick frying pan over a medium-high heat and pour in the oil. Once the oil is hot, place the coated tofu around the pan evenly and fry for about 12 minutes, gently turning the slices and frying on each side until just golden and crispy. Turn off the heat, remove the tofu from the pan and place on a plate lined with paper towels to absorb any excess oil.

To serve, arrange the tofu on a serving plate and drizzle the sauce over. Garnish with micro herbs and serve immediately.

핫도그

SERVES 6

Prep time: 14 minutes
Total time: 30 minutes

140g (scant 1¼ cups) strong white
    bread flour
50g (¼ cup) Asian rice flour
2 tbsp granulated sugar
1 tsp sea or kosher salt
120ml (½ cup) whole milk, plus extra
    as needed
¾ tsp fast-action dried yeast
1 large egg, at room temperature
1.5–2.6l (6–11 cups) vegetable or
    other neutral oil
3 good-quality hot dog sausages,
    halved lengthwise and cut into
    approximately 7cm (2½in) lengths
450g (1lb) block of low-moisture
    mozzarella cheese, cut into 7 x 2cm
    (2½ x ¾in) pieces, roughly the same
    thickness as the sausages

For the Coating (choose one)
50g (1 cup) panko breadcrumbs
100g (3½oz) packet of thin instant
    ramen noodles, crushed into very
    small pieces
330g (12oz) frozen crinkle-cut French
    fries, diced into 1cm (½in) cubes

For the Toppings (optional)
sugar, ketchup, mustard, mayonnaise,
    sriracha, curry powder

You will need six wooden chopsticks
    or 25cm (10in) skewers

Totally Satisfying Korean Corn Dogs

Hatdogeu

Korean corn dogs are all the rage, with lines stretching down the block at vendors. Despite the name, there's no corn involved – instead, they feature a delicious chewy wheat and rice flour dough encasing gooey mozzarella or a juicy hot dog (sometimes both!). Be sure to use plain Asian rice flour and not glutinous (sweet) or Western rice flour, which are different products. Get creative with your toppings and enjoy!

In a large bowl, whisk together the flours, sugar and salt. Set aside.

Tip the milk into a medium heatproof bowl and warm in the microwave on high for about 1 minute, until it reaches 43°C (110°F). Whisk in the yeast and set aside for 5 minutes, or until it starts to bubble. Once bubbling, whisk the egg into the milk mixture, then add the flour mixture in parts, mixing well after each addition. The dough should be sticky and thick. If the batter is too wet, add a bit more bread flour. Pour the batter into a wide, tall cup.

Fill a large saucepan (choose one that is wider than the skewers or chopsticks you are using) with the oil so that it reaches 10cm (4in) up the sides of the pan and, using a kitchen thermometer, heat to 165°C (330°F).

Spread your chosen coating across a large plate. Set aside.

Spear the hot dog pieces onto the chopsticks or skewers through the centre of the hot dog lengthwise, taking care to stay in the middle of the sausage. Push them down just far enough to make room for the cheese pieces on top. Skewer the cheese pieces on the top end of the chopsticks or skewers, again through the centre of the block lengthwise, just enough to be secure.

Dip the filled skewers one at a time into the batter while spinning the skewer to coat the hot dogs and cheese evenly, removing any excess.

Immediately roll the battered skewers in panko or instant noodles, or stick the diced French fries to them. As soon as they're coated, carefully place the coated corn dogs in the heated oil.

Fry the corn dogs for 3–5 minutes until puffed and golden brown, turning as necessary. Remove the corn dogs from the oil and place on a wire rack set over a tray to allow any excess oil to drip off.

Sprinkle on sugar, or drizzle with the sauces (if using) and serve immediately.

콜리플라워 튀김

My Favourite Korean Fried Cauliflower

Kollipeullawo Twigim

SERVES 2–4

This version of Korean fried cauliflower is a total hit at my restaurant, Seoul Bird. I tend to order it more than the fried chicken! For a quicker prep, use pre-cut cauliflower available in microwavable steamer bags. To ensure a light and crispy texture, use ice-cold water in the batter – this temperature contrast minimises oil absorption during frying. These golden florets are addictive and are sure to disappear first at your next dinner party.

Prep time: 10 minutes
Total time: 30 minutes

sea or kosher salt
450g (1lb) cauliflower florets
35g (¼ cup) cornflour (cornstarch)

For the Batter

35g (¼ cup) cornflour (cornstarch)
1 tbsp potato starch
2 tbsp plain (all-purpose) flour
1¼ tsp onion powder
1¼ tsp garlic powder
¼ tsp baking powder
½ tbsp sea or kosher salt
1.5–2.6l (6–11 cups) vegetable or other neutral oil

Prepare an ice bath in a large bowl.

Fill a large saucepan with water, add 1–2 tbsp of salt (depending on how big your pan is) and bring to the boil. Add the cauliflower florets and blanch for 2 minutes. Drain the cauliflower and transfer to the ice bath. Drain again and shake off the excess water thoroughly. Alternatively, put the cauliflower in a large heatproof bowl with 60–120ml (¼–½ cup) water. Place a heatproof plate on top and microwave on high for 4–6 minutes. You can also buy the cauliflower into a steamer bag and cook according to the packet instructions. Once the cauliflower is cooked, shock in the ice bath as above and then drain, shaking off the excess water.

To Serve

1 red chilli, preferably Korean but a Fresno will also work, thinly sliced
1 spring onion (scallion), thinly sliced on a bias
2 tbsp Gochujang Mayo (see page 191)

Pour the cornflour onto a large plate, and place a wire rack over a tray. Dust the cauliflower florets with the cornflour, shaking the excess off well, then place the coated florets on the rack.

Next, make the batter mix. In a large bowl, whisk together all of the ingredients, then add about 150ml (scant ⅔ cup) very cold water and whisk again. The consistency of the batter should be like paint.

Next, place a large, wide, heavy-based saucepan that is at least 13cm (5in) deep on the stove. Pour in about 5cm (2in) of vegetable oil and, using a kitchen thermometer, heat to 200°C (400°F). Place a wire rack over a tray and put it next to the frying pan.

Using tongs, dip the cauliflower florets one by one into the wet batter mix and fry for 1–2 minutes until golden brown. You'll need to hold each floret in the hot oil for a few seconds before releasing to prevent it sticking to the bottom. Fry the cauliflower in batches without overcrowding the pan; you don't want them to touch. Do not let the oil temperature dip below 180°C (350°F) to ensure crispiness.

Transfer each batch of cooked cauliflower to the rack with a slotted spoon. Once all it is cooked, place in a wide serving bowl and sprinkle over the chilli and spring onion. Serve immediately with gochujang mayo on the side.

길거리 토스트

Korean Street Toast

Gilgeori Toseuteu

MAKES 1 SANDWICH

Prep time: 14 minutes
Total time: 30 minutes

60g (1 cup) packaged coleslaw mix or 40g (1½oz) white cabbage, thinly sliced and 20g (¾oz) carrot, peeled and julienned
2 spring onions (scallions), julienned
1 tbsp chopped parsley
½ tsp sea or kosher salt
¼ tsp freshly ground black pepper
1 large egg
3 tbsp salted butter, plus extra as needed
2 slices uyu sikppang (Korean milk bread)
1 tsp granulated sugar
1–2 slices Monterey Jack or mild Cheddar
2–4 slices cured ham
2–4 slices salami

To Serve
1–2 tbsp ketchup
1–2 tbsp Kewpie mayonnaise (or your favourite mayonnaise)

This sando is the breakfast of champions, hailing from the streets of Seoul. I do encourage you to try this hearty toastie – it's packed with everything you need for a soul-satisfying breakfast or lunch. If you can't find uyi sikppang, shokupan (Japanese milk bread) or good-quality white bread make suitable alternatives. Feel free to omit the sugar if you'd like to keep this sandwich completely savoury, but it does add a nice zing!

In a large bowl, toss together the coleslaw mix or cabbage and carrot, spring onions, parsley, salt and pepper. Massage the vegetables well with your hands and set aside to soften for 1 minute.

Next, add the egg and mix well with a spoon.

Heat a large non-stick frying pan over a medium heat, then add about 1 tbsp of the butter. Melt the butter and swirl the pan to coat it. Add the bread and let it soak up the butter and toast until golden brown and a little crispy. Add another tbsp of butter, flip the bread and cook the other side until toasted and crisp.

When the bread is toasted on both sides, remove it from the pan, put on a plate and sprinkle the sugar evenly over one side of each slice.

Heat the remaining butter in the same pan over a medium heat. Carefully spoon in the cabbage mixture and, while it cooks, roughly shape it to the size of the toast. Cook for 2–3 minutes until golden brown, then flip it over with a non-stick spatula and add more butter if needed.

Place the cheese, ham and salami on top of the cabbage mixture and cook for about 2–3 minutes until the cabbage mixture turns golden brown underneath and it has formed a rough patty

Place the cooked cabbage patty with the ham and cheese on top of the bread, then spread the ketchup and mayonnaise as you like. Put the other slice of toast, sugared side down, on top. Cut in half, as you prefer, and serve immediately.

간장연두부

SERVES 1–2

Prep time: 10 minutes
Total time: 10 minutes

2 tbsp soy sauce
2 tbsp roasted sesame oil
2 tsp roasted sesame seeds
1 tsp casater (superfine) sugar
½ tsp grated garlic
¼ tsp freshly ground black pepper
½ tsp gochugaru (Korean chilli flakes)
   (optional)
2 spring onions (scallions), white and
   green parts, sliced thinly on a bias
340g (12oz) silken tofu

Soothing Silken Tofu

Ganjangyeondubu

I have an absolute passion for tofu. In East Asian cuisine, it holds its own esteemed status and isn't merely regarded as a sentence of culinary exile. This effortless, simple dish often finds its way onto my lunch plate, occasionally adorned with chopped kimchi for an extra kick. I've suggested using silken tofu but feel free to choose whichever variety suits your palate best; this recipe seamlessly accommodates them all, whether you prefer it served piping hot or refreshingly cold.

In a small bowl, whisk together the soy sauce, sesame oil, sesame seeds, sugar, garlic, pepper and gochugaru (if using) until the sugar is completely dissolved. Stir in half of the spring onions.

Place the tofu in a serving bowl and break apart gently using a spoon or cut into slices. Pour the sauce over the tofu. Sprinkle over the remaining spring onions and serve.

To serve hot, simply place the tofu in a heatproof dish and then heat in a microwave for about 3 minutes, or in a steamer for 3–4 minutes, drain then top with the sauce.

버섯파전

SERVES 4

Prep time: 14 minutes
Total time: 30 minutes

90g (¾ cup) buchim garu (Korean
    pancake mix)
90g (¾ cup) twigim garu (Korean
    frying mix)
vegetable or other neutral oil,
    for frying
80g (2¾oz) shiitake mushrooms,
    destemmed and sliced about 5mm
    (¼in) thick
50g (1¾oz) oyster mushrooms, torn
    into 5mm (¼in) pieces
65g (2½oz) enoki mushrooms,
    trimmed and broken apart
4 spring onions (scallions), thinly
    sliced
sea or kosher salt
freshly ground black pepper

To Serve
Jeon Dipping Sauce (see page 195)

Crispy Mushroom & Spring Onion Pancakes

Beoseot Pajeon

My mother had a knack for whipping up pajeon to use up all the random leftovers lurking in the fridge. Don't hesitate to toss in any seasonal vegetables or meats – even those humble cured meats and cold-cuts find their place here! Making jeon on a rainy day is a cherished tradition, as the sizzle of these savoury pancakes echoes the gentle patter of raindrops outside. In this version, feel free to swap out the mushroom varieties for whatever happens to be on hand. For those pressed for time, opting for shop-bought, pre-cut mushrooms is a convenient shortcut worth taking.

In a large bowl, whisk together the buchim garu and twigim garu. Gradually add roughly 355ml (1½ cups) water to make a thickish wet batter mix. Set aside. This batter can be made up to a day in advance, just keep it chilled in the fridge.

Preheat a large non-stick frying pan over a medium-high heat, then drizzle in about 2 tbsp oil and add the mushrooms. Sauté the mushrooms until slightly dried out but still soft, about 7–8 minutes. Season to taste. Once done, remove the mushrooms from the pan, draining away any excess oil, and mix the mushrooms and the spring onions into the batter mix.

Clean out the frying pan, place over a medium heat, and drizzle in 3–4 tbsp oil. Using a ladle, scoop in half of the batter mix. Cook for 3–4 minutes until the edges are crispy and golden brown, then carefully flip and cook for an additional 3–4 minutes. Add more oil as necessary and fry until the edges are a browned, flipping as necessary. Transfer to a paper towel-lined plate or a wire rack set over a baking sheet. Repeat with the remaining batter.

Place on a large serving platter and cut into bite-sized pieces. Serve immediately with the dipping sauce on the side.

Courgette Stir-fry

호박볶음

Hobak Bokkeum

SERVES 4

Prep time: 7 minutes
Total time: 15 minutes

310g (11oz) courgette (zucchini),
  preferably Korean courgettes or
  aehobaks
1 tbsp roasted sesame oil
½ tbsp grated garlic
1½ tsp saeu-jeot (salted shrimp) or
  fish sauce
1 tsp roasted sesame seeds, crushed
½ spring onion (scallion), thinly sliced
sea or kosher salt
freshly ground black pepper

Try to find Korean courgette (aehobak) with vibrant yellow insides to make this delectable banchan. They boast a firmer and sweeter texture compared to their Western counterparts. Use a mandoline to thinly slice the courgettes to ensure even cooking, and feel free to swap out the salted shrimp with light soy sauce to make this dish plant forward.

Halve the courgette lengthwise, then slice crosswise into 1cm (½in) thick half-moon pieces.

Place the sesame oil and garlic into a medium non-stick frying pan. Cook over a low heat until just softened, about 1 minute. Add the courgette slices and cook, stirring often with a wooden spoon, until just wilted, about 2–3 minutes. Add the saeu-jeot and 1 tbsp water. Cook for 3–4 minutes until the courgette is softened, but not losing its shape. Add the sesame seeds and spring onion, then toss well. Remove from the heat and season with salt and pepper to taste.

콜슬로

SERVES 4

Prep time: 15 minutes
Total time: 15 minutes

For the Slaw

225g (8oz) red cabbage
120g (4oz) red onion
160g (5¾oz) carrot
100g (3½oz) mu (Korean radish) or
  daikon radish

For the Citrus-soy Dressing

3 tbsp lemon juice
1⅓ tbsp mirim
1⅔ tbsp roasted sesame oil
1⅓ tbsp soy sauce
1 large garlic clove, grated
½–1 tsp gochugaru (Korean chilli
  flakes), or more to taste
sea or kosher salt

Refreshing Asian Coleslaw with Citrus-soy Dressing

Kolseullo

This quick and refreshing slaw has always been on the menu at Seoul Bird. I adore the vibrant dressing as a tangy departure from the usual creamy mayonnaise-based coleslaws. Feel free to use any type of cabbage – Chinese leaf (Napa), Savoy or green. Save time by using a food processor or opt for pre-cut packaged coleslaw mix to whip up this side salad in no time.

Very finely grate or shred the red cabbage, onion, carrot and daikon in a food processor, on a mandoline or using a julienne peeler. Place all the shredded vegetables in a large bowl and mix well.

In a separate bowl, whisk together the dressing ingredients and then add salt to taste. Dress the slaw, tossing well, and serve immediately.

감자샐러드

SERVES 8–10

Prep time: 16 minutes
Total time: 30 minutes

3 large eggs
2 sweetcorn cobs or 220g (1¼ cups)
 sweetcorn kernels
60g (2oz) carrots, peeled and
 julienned and then cut into
 3mm (⅛in) dice
1 echalion shallot, or 2 small round
 shallots, peeled and quartered and
 placed in a bowl of cold water to
 dampen any sharpness
120g (4oz) cucumber, deseeded and
 cut into 5mm (¼in) dice
60g (¼ cup) Kewpie mayonnaise (or
 your favourite mayonnaise)
935g (4 cups) chilled premade
 mashed potato
sea or kosher salt
freshly ground black pepper
1 tsp caster (superfine) sugar
 (optional)
1 tsp sagwa-sikcho (Korean apple
 vinegar) or rice vinegar (optional)

The Best Korean Potato Salad

Gamja Saelleodeu

Korean potato salad really is a thing! Even though it seems random among the other plates of banchan, you'll often find this creamy side dish served in restaurants. Serve these spuds with Korean barbecue or as a lunchtime snack. When using leftover or shop-bought mash, opt for plain varieties to avoid altering the flavour, and remove any pats of butter on top. This recipe makes plenty, but it is so good – perfect for sandos or croquettes!

Fill a large saucepan with water, place over a high heat and add the eggs and sweetcorn cobs (if using tinned corn kernels, there's no need to cook them). Make sure the corn is fully submerged. Bring to the boil, then lower to a simmer. Using tongs, remove the corn once cooked, about 3–4 minutes, and set aside to cool on a plate. After a further 9–10 minutes, remove the eggs using a slotted spoon and place into a small bowl.

Cool the eggs under cold running water, then peel and cut into 1cm (½in) dice. Place the diced eggs into a large bowl.

Using a sharp knife, cut the corn kernels off the cobs, and place into the bowl with the eggs. If using tinned corn, drain, rinse well with water through a colander and shake away any excess liquid, then add to the eggs.

Add the finely diced carrots to the eggs and corn. Remove the shallots from the bowl of water and finely chop into 3mm (⅛in) pieces, then add to the bowl. Add the cucumber and mayonnaise.

Finally, add the mashed potatoes, mix well and season with salt and pepper to taste.

If you want your salad a bit sweeter, add the caster sugar. To add more tang, add the sagwa-sikcho.

To store leftovers, put in an airtight container in the fridge; it will stay fresh for 2–3 days.

Tips

Feel free to use tinned corn.

Buy packaged grated (shredded) carrots or use a julienne peeler to save time.

로마네스코 버섯
참깨 샐러드

Colourful Romanesco, Mushroom & Sesame Salad

Beoseot Romaneseuko Chamkkae Saelleodeu

SERVES 4–6

Prep time: 28 minutes
Total time: 30 minutes

½–1 tsp sea or kosher salt, plus extra
    to taste
2 tbsp roasted sesame seeds
1 tbsp roasted sesame oil
1 tbsp soy sauce
1 tbsp sagwa-sikcho (Korean apple
    vinegar) or rice vinegar
2 garlic cloves, grated
150g (5½oz) romanesco florets, cut
    into 2cm (1in) pieces
80g (2¾oz) fresh shiitake
    mushrooms, sliced
110g (3¾oz) button mushrooms,
    stems trimmed and thinly sliced
½ bunch chives, cut into 2cm (1in)
    pieces

To Serve
black sesame seeds (optional)

You will adore this light and fresh-tasting banchan (side dish). If you cannot find romanesco, try making this salad with regular broccoli or cauliflower. You can also use other mushrooms, but choose ones that are tasty when eaten raw.

Bring a large saucepan of water to the boil and add the salt, depending on how large your saucepan is. Prepare an ice bath in a large bowl.

Meanwhile, in a large bowl, stir together the sesame seeds, sesame oil, soy sauce, sagwa-sikcho, garlic and a little salt to taste. Set the dressing aside.

Blanch the romanesco in the boiling water until crisp-tender, 1½–2 minutes, then drain, shock in the ice bath and drain well again.

Add the blanched romanesco, mushrooms and chives to the bowl with the dressing and toss to coat. Transfer to a platter, sprinkle with black sesame seeds (if using) and serve.

파무침

SERVES 6

Prep time: 20 minutes
Total time: 20 minutes

8 spring onions (scallions), cut into
   13cm (5in) pieces
½ small red onion, thinly sliced
2 tbsp soy sauce
3½ tbsp sagwa-sikcho (Korean apple
   vinegar) or rice vinegar
1 tbsp roasted sesame oil
2 tsp gochugaru (Korean chilli flakes)
2 tbsp caster (superfine) sugar
sea or kosher salt

Sexy Spring Onion Salad

Pa Muchim

I can eat bucketloads of this sexy, curly spring onion salad whenever I indulge in Korean barbecue. Its spicy, sweet, sour and tangy flavours are simply irresistible! It's the quintessential accompaniment to any grilled meats, infusing each bite with a burst of freshness. Plus, this soy vinaigrette doubles as a fantastic dressing for any salad – I always keep a jar of it in my fridge. The curly spring onions (scallions) make a great garnish and you'll find them topping a number of recipes in this book.

Place the spring onions and red onion in a large bowl of iced water and soak until the spring onions curl up, at least 5 minutes, or up to 2 hours in the fridge. When ready to serve, drain well and spin in a salad spinner or pat dry.

In a medium bowl, whisk together the soy sauce, sagwa-sikcho, sesame oil, gochugaru, sugar and a pinch of salt until the sugar dissolves. Add the spring onions and red onion, toss to coat and serve.

KIMCHI

&

—PICKLES

사과김치

———

MAKES 600G
(4 CUPS)

Prep time: 25 minutes
Total time: 25 minutes

225g (8oz) Fuji, Pink Lady or
   Honeycrisp apples
225g (8oz) green apples
½ brown (yellow) onion, chopped
   into 2.5cm (1in) pieces
3 spring onions (scallions), trimmed,
   split lengthwise, then cut into 5cm
   (2in) pieces
¾ tsp sea or kosher salt
¾ tsp gochugaru (Korean chilli flakes)
1½ tsp anchovy sauce or fish sauce
1½ tsp grated garlic
¾ tsp grated ginger
2¼ tsp maesil cheong (plum extract)
¾ tsp saeu-jeot (salted shrimp)

Fresh Apple Kimchi

Sagwa Kimchi

My aunt makes this very refreshing and rather addictive kimchi in the autumn (fall) when apples are crisp and sweet. Choose firm fruit, as the apples will start to break down after 2–3 days. But I guarantee that this irresistible dish won't stick around that long – it's so tasty!

Peel and chop the apples into 1.5cm (¾in) pieces.

In a large bowl, mix together the apples, onion and spring onions.

In a smaller bowl, mix together the salt, gochugaru, anchovy sauce or fish sauce, garlic, ginger, maesil cheong and saeu-jeot. Add the sauce to the apples, onion and spring onions and mix well.

Eat immediately or place in a jar or non-reactive container, store in the fridge and consume within 3 days.

My Master Recipe: Cabbage Kimchi

Baechu Kimchi

MAKES 3 HEADS OF KIMCHI

Active time: 30 minutes
Total time: 7–10 days, for
   fermentation

230–250g (8¼–9oz) Korean solar sea
   salt or similar coarse salt
220g (7¾oz) baechu (Chinese leaf/
   Napa cabbage) (about 3 heads)
430g (15¼oz) garlic cloves, peeled
200g (7oz) ginger, peeled
105g (scant ½ cup) saeu-jeot (salted
   shrimp)
200g (scant 1 cup) good-quality
   maesil cheong (plum extract), plus
   extra as needed
105g (scant ½ cup) Korean anchovy
   sauce or fish sauce
300g (1½ cups) gochugaru (Korean
   chilli flakes), coarsely ground (or to
   taste, depending on how spicy the
   brand is)
200g (scant 1 cup) Anchovy Dashi
   Stock (see page 192)
300g (1½ cups) packaged grated
   (shredded) carrots
220g (1 cup) buchu (Chinese chives)
   (or spring onions/scallions), thinly
   sliced into 7.5cm (3in) pieces

Tips

To make the kimchi vegan, omit the
saeu-jeot and use Vegetarian Dashi
Stock (see page 193).

You can spread the chilli paste on the
half heads: it takes longer, but the
result is beautiful wedges of cabbage.
Start from the inner most leaf,
coating both sides and make your
way out to the largest leaves.

A Korean cookbook is not complete without a kimchi recipe. Although kimchi takes weeks to ferment, the active prep time is not long at all. Although kimchi tastes the best once it has had time to ferment (I usually give mine 2 weeks), you can eat it 'fresh' on the day of making so feel free to enjoy it whenever you like. Once it becomes very ripe – it is best to use in soups and stews such as the Warming Kimchi Stew (see page 156), but it also works well in the Kimchi and Pork Sausage Pancakes (see page 93) and Kimchi Fried Rice (see pages 132–34). I created this recipe to lead a 100-person 'kimjang' (kimchi-making party) for the Korean Ambassador to the UK. Everyone took home a jar of their own kimchi; it was brilliant! I recommend using natural or organic ingredients where you can, as it reallys improve the flavour of the kimchi.

First, brine the cabbage. Fill a large container with warm water, add the salt and mix until completely dissolved. The water should taste salty, but not overly salty. Allow the salted water to cool to room temperature.

Note: weigh your water and use about 10–15% of the weight in salt, depending on preference. I usually use about 2l (½ gallon) water and 230g –250g (8¼–9oz) coarse Korean solar sea salt, but not all salt is the same saltiness, so taste it.

Meanwhile, trim and discard the outer leaves of the cabbage. Cut the cabbages in half by slicing from the core downwards (to keep the top leaves full and intact) and pull the cabbages apart gently. If you are using a large head of cabbage, quarter in the same way.

Place the cabbages in the cooled salted water, cut side up, and place a heavy bowl or plate on top to fully submerge them in the brine. Leave overnight at room temperature.

Place the garlic, ginger, saeu-jeot, maesil cheong and anchovy sauce or fish sauce in a food processor and blend until smooth. Transfer to a bowl, then add the gochugaru and mix well. Add some stock to loosen the mixture and make the paste thick but spreadable. Taste and adjust the amount of maesil cheong or gochugaru as desired.

Mix in the carrots and Chinese chives or spring onions. Cover with cling film (plastic wrap) and chill in the fridge.

The next day, remove the cabbage from the brine and drain well by placing cut side down in a large colander placed over a deep plate or in a sink. Taste one of the leaves; it should be pleasantly salty and palatable (if it is too salty, rinse and soak in cold water for about 20 minutes). Rinse the cabbage under cold water and drain well.

Place the cabbage sections on a cutting board. Using a sharp knife, cut the cabbage into 5cm (2in) wide pieces, and put into a large non-reactive container with an airtight lid. Slice the roots of the cabbage about 5mm (¼in) thick and add to the container too.

After cutting up two of the cabbage wedges, spoon in some of the chilli paste. Repeat, layering the cabbage and the chilli paste in the container until done. Then, using gloved hands or a large spoon, mix the cabbage and the paste in the container until all of the cabbage is well coated and red in colour. Press the cabbage down in the container so it is flat on top. Close the lid.

Leave to ferment at room temperature (18°C/65°F) for 7–10 days, then place in the fridge. Depending on how warm your room is, you may shorten the room temperature fermentation by 1–2 days.

Make sure you 'burp' your kimchi and release the air pressure in the container daily. Otherwise, it may explode!

배추겉절이

SERVES 2–3

Prep time: 30 minutes
Total time: 30 minutes

1kg (2lb oz) baechu (Chinese leaf/
Napa cabbage)
1 tbsp coarse sea or kosher salt
25g (¼ cup) gochugaru (Korean chilli
flakes)
1 tbsp caster (superfine) sugar
1 tbsp saeu-jeot (salted shrimp)
1 tbsp fish sauce
1 tbsp grated garlic
½ brown (yellow) onion, sliced into
5mm (¼in) pieces
3 spring onions (scallions), halved
lengthwise, then into 5cm (2in)
pieces

To Serve
roasted sesame oil (optional)

Fresh Cabbage Kimchi Salad

Baechu Geotjeori

This recipe feels more like a salad, as it is a type of kimchi that is eaten immediately without any fermentation. There are many variations of this fresh form of kimchi – crisp salted cabbage tossed with an aromatic garlicky dressing. This is a simple version that can be served as part of your banchan spread or alongside Umma's Clam Knife-cut Noodles (see page 143).

Trim off the bottom of the cabbage and thoroughly clean the leaves with cold water, discarding any wilted or bruised ones. Drain well, shake off any excess water and chop the leaves into bite-size pieces, about 5cm (2in) wide. Place the cut cabbage in a large colander set over a bowl, toss the cabbage with the salt and spread out evenly over the colander. Set aside for 10 minutes.

Meanwhile, in a separate bowl, mix together the gochugaru, sugar, saeu-jeot, fish sauce and garlic.

After the cabbage has been sitting for 10 minutes, drain off any excess liquid. Mix the cabbage with the sauce, onion and spring onions. Drizzle with the sesame oil (if using). Serve immediately.

무생채

———

SERVES 2–4

Prep time: 10 minutes
Total time: 10 minutes

175g (6oz) mu (Korean radish) or
   daikon radish, peeled and julienned
1½ tbsp rice or distilled white vinegar
1½ tbsp caster (superfine) sugar
2 tsp gochugaru (Korean chilli flakes)
1 small garlic clove, grated
1 spring onion (scallion), thinly sliced
1 tsp sea or kosher salt

<u>To Serve</u>
roasted sesame seeds

The Easiest Pickled Radish Banchan

Musaengchae

I always keep a jar of this zippy and fresh radish side dish in my fridge. It's ideal as a topping for Bountiful Bibimbap (see page 135) or for Korean barbecue in ssam leaf wraps (see pages 78, 90, 96 and 110). Depending on the season, you may need to adjust the amount of sugar, as radishes can be more bitter when out of season. It is so easy to make and such a crowd pleaser – you'll want to eat this sweet, tangy and refreshing pickle with everything!

In a large bowl, stir together all the ingredients until the radish is evenly coated in the sauce and the sugar dissolves. Sprinkle with sesame seeds and then serve immediately or cover and chill until ready to eat.

오이양파장아찌

**MAKES 1 X 1L
(34OZ) JAR**

Prep time: 13 minutes
Total time: 15 minutes, plus at least
 8 hours at room temperature
 overnight, then chilled in the fridge
 for 1 day

340g (3 cups) firm Korean pickling
 cucumbers (or another cucumber
 variety suitable for pickling, such as
 Kirby or Persian cucumbers), sliced
 into 5mm (¼in) slices
170g (1 cup) chopped brown (yellow)
 onion
1 green chilli, preferably Korean but a
 jalapeño will also work, sliced into
 5mm (¼in) slices
160ml (⅔ cup) soy sauce
50g (¼ cup) caster (superfine) sugar
120ml (½ cup) rice vinegar

Soy-pickled Cucumbers & Onions

Oiyangpajang-aji

Everyone loves a pickled cucumber – and with an umami-filled soy sauce pickling brine, you can't go wrong. These crunchy cukes are served as banchan and pair particularly well with pajeon – you can even use the pickling liquid as a dipping sauce for jeon (see pages 40 and 114) or mandu (see page 95).

Place the vegetables into a heatproof jar or plastic storage container with a lid.

Put 120ml (½ cup) water in a small saucepan, add the soy sauce and sugar, then bring to the boil, whisking to dissolve the sugar. Remove from the heat, leave to cool and then add the vinegar.

Pour the soy sauce mixture over the vegetables, making sure they are all submerged.

Close the lid tightly and leave to pickle at room temperature overnight. Chill in the fridge for 1 day, then consume within 1 month.

오이무침

MAKES 1 X 1L
(34OZ) JAR

Prep time: 30 minutes
Total time: 30 minutes

1 tbsp gochugaru (Korean chilli
flakes), or to taste
1 tbsp fish sauce
2 tsp rice vinegar
2 tsp roasted sesame oil
1 tbsp caster (superfine) sugar
2 large garlic cloves, grated
450g (1lb) small cucumbers,
preferably Korean cucumbers but
Kirby or Persian cucumbers will
also work
2 spring onions (scallions), thinly
sliced

Spicy Pickled Cucumbers

Oi Muchim

This quick zingy and spicy pickle is great to eat with just about anything.
Use fresh and firm cucumbers to ensure a crunchy and revitalising bite.
This recipe also works well with English cucumbers. However, if using
hothouse cukes (or any variety with thicker skin) make sure to peel it off,
and scrape out the seeds.

Put the gochugaru, fish sauce, rice vinegar, sesame oil, sugar and garlic into
a large bowl and mix well, making sure the sugar is dissolved. Slice each
cucumber into 5mm (¼in) thick round pieces and place in the same bowl
along with the spring onions and gently toss to coat.

This dish can be eaten immediately, or covered and allowed to pickle and
macerate further at room temperature or in the fridge for up to 2 days.

수박껍질피클

Watermelon Rind Pickle

Subak Kkeobjjil Pikeul

MAKES 1 X 1L
(34OZ) JAR

Prep time: 26 minutes
Total time: 30 minutes, plus 1 hour
30 minutes to cool to room
temperature, then chilled overnight
in the fridge

450g (1lb) watermelon rind
180ml (¾ cup) rice vinegar
100g (½ cup) caster (superfine) sugar
2 tsp pickling salt
2 tbsp thinly sliced ginger
2 garlic cloves, thinly sliced
½ tsp white peppercorns
½ tsp gochugaru (Korean chilli flakes)

In today's world of minimising waste, this pickle ingeniously repurposes what's typically discarded: watermelon rinds. I typically opt for small watermelons to avoid the challenge of handling larger ones, but if using full-sized melons, ensure the rind's thickness doesn't exceed 1cm (½in). Once you've savoured the delightful blend of sour and sweet in these pickles, you'll never view watermelon rinds as mere scraps again.

Trim the watermelon rind well, removing all of the green part with a sharp vegetable peeler and most of the pink watermelon flesh with a knife. Cut the rind into 2.5cm (1in) squares, making sure the rind doesn't exceed 1cm (½in) thick.

In a large saucepan, combine the vinegar, sugar, salt, ginger, garlic, peppercorns, gochugaru and 360ml (1½ cups) of water. Place over a medium-high heat and bring to the boil, then add the watermelon. Bring to the boil again, then remove from the heat and place in heatproof containers or sterilized Kilner (Mason) jars. Allow to cool to room temperature without a lid (about 1 hour 30 minutes), then put on the lid and place in the fridge. The pickles should be ready to eat the next day and will keep for about a month.

ALL
ABOUT —

CHICKEN

찜닭

SERVES 4

Total time: 10 minutes
Total time: 30 minutes

115g (4oz) dangmyeon (sweet potato
  noodles)
vegetable or other neutral oil, for
  cooking
900g (2lb) boneless skinless chicken
  thighs, quartered (about 5cm/2in
  pieces)
105g (1 cup) frozen pearl onions
225g (8oz) baby potatoes (or larger
  potatoes cut into 2.5cm/1in pieces)
150g (5½oz) baby carrots
6 spring onions (scallions), trimmed,
  split lengthwise and cut into 5cm
  (2in) pieces
2 red Korean chillis, sliced on
  a bias

For the Sauce

60ml (¼ cup) soy sauce
5 garlic cloves, grated
1 tbsp fish sauce
2 tbsp mirim
2 tbsp dark brown sugar
1 tsp grated ginger

To Serve (optional)

2 tsp roasted sesame oil
freshly ground black pepper
black sesame seeds
'sexy' spring onions (scallions) (follow
  step 1 on page 50)
silgochu (chilli threads)
steamed shortgrain white rice

The Coziest Braised Chicken Stew

Jjimdak

Korea gets bitterly cold during the winter months and thus a tradition of hearty stews evolved. I have cut prep time here by using all prepared baby vegetables from a bag, and they look cute too! Searing the chicken is optional, as it does take time, but it will bring more colour and flavour to the stew. Serve with a bowl of hot steaming rice on the side and you'll feel cozy from the inside out.

In a large bowl, place the noodles in warm water. Set aside and leave to soak while you make the rest of the recipe.

In a small bowl, whisk together all the sauce ingredients along with 350ml (1½ cups) water, making sure the sugar has dissolved. Set aside.

Place a large, wide, heavy-based saucepan over a high heat. Drizzle 2–3 tbsp vegetable oil into the pan and add the chicken to brown in one layer for 3–4 minutes or in batches, if you like. Add the sauce, onions, potatoes and carrots to the chicken, and bring to the boil. Boil for 10 minutes, or until the potatoes are tender. Drain and add the noodles, stir, and cook for an additional 5 minutes until the noodles become translucent and the sauce thickens slightly. Add the spring onions and chillis and stir, then turn off the heat. To finish, drizzle with sesame oil, add a few grinds of black pepper, then scatter with the sesame seeds, spring onions and chilli threads (if using) on top. Serve immediately as the noodles will continue to soak up liquid as the stew sits.

닭떡꼬치

Prep time: 17 minutes
Total time: 25 minutes

12 pieces of tteok (Korean rice
   cakes), jorangi tteok or star-/
   heart-shaped tteok preferred,
   but you can use any shape besides
   the coin-shaped sliced type)
2 tbsp mirim
1 tbsp soy sauce
1 tbsp roasted sesame oil
1 large garlic clove, grated
225g (8oz) boneless skinless chicken
   thighs, cut crosswise into a total of
   12 x 2cm (¾in) wide pieces
vegetable or other neutral oil,
   for cooking
sea or kosher salt

For the Gochujang Hot Honey Sauce

60g (¼ cup) runny honey
1 tbsp gochujang (Korean chilli paste)
1 tsp soy sauce
1 tsp sea or kosher salt
½ tsp rice vinegar
1 tsp roasted sesame oil

To Serve

chives, thinly sliced (optional)

You will also need six metal or
   bamboo skewers (the latter will
   need soaking in water for at least 10
   minutes).

Appa's Chicken & Rice Cake Skewers

Dak Tteokkochi

One of my father's favourite things to eat is tteok, Korean rice cakes. I inherited his love for these chewy, toothsome snacks, especially when simply grilled and brushed with a sweet and spicy glaze. Skewers of tteok are a popular street food in Korea. Students love noshing on these sticks after school, and evening revellers pick them up after a night of drinking.

Place the tteok in a small heatproof bowl and soak in boiling water for 30–60 seconds until just soft. Drain and set aside.

In a medium bowl, combine the mirim, soy sauce, sesame oil and garlic. Add the chicken and toss to coat. Set aside at room temperature.

In another small bowl, mix together the ingredients for the gochujang hot honey sauce. Set aside.

Preheat a griddle pan over a medium-high heat. Pat the tteok dry with paper towels. Place two pieces of marinated chicken and two pieces of drained tteok on a skewer. Repeat with the remaining skewers, ending up with six skewers.

Lightly brush the griddle with vegetable oil and gently place the skewers on it. Cook, flipping once, for 2 minutes each side until the tteok is toasted and the chicken is fully cooked. Repeat until all the skewers are cooked. Brush the tteok with the gochujang hot honey sauce and serve with the remaining sauce on the side. Finish with a sprinkling of chopped chives (if using).

춘천 닭갈비

SERVES 2–3

Prep time: 18 minutes
Total time: 30 minutes

150g (5½oz) garae-tteok (Korean cylinder-shaped rice cakes)
450g (1lb) boneless skin-on chicken thighs, cut into 2.5cm (1in) pieces
2 tbsp vegetable or other neutral oil
170g (3 cups) packaged coleslaw mix or shredded cabbage and carrot
1 brown (yellow) onion, cut into 5mm (¼in) slices
2 spring onions (scallions), cut into 5cm (2in) pieces
½ goguma (Korean sweet potato), peeled and halved lengthwise, then cut into 5mm (¼in) slices

For the Chicken Marinade

2 tsp soy sauce
3 tbsp gochujang (Korean chilli paste)
2 tbsp gochugaru (Korean chilli flakes), or to taste
2 tbsp rice syrup or funny buchim garu (Korean frying mix)
3 tbsp mirim
2 tbsp grated garlic
1 tbsp grated ginger
1 tbsp roasted sesame oil
1 tbsp Korean curry powder
2 tsp freshly ground black pepper

To Serve

10–13 kkaennip (perilla leaves), cut into 5mm (¼in) strips

Chuncheon-style Chicken

Chuncheon Dakgalbi

Spicy food lovers – this dish is for you. Originally from Chuncheon, this dish is now eaten throughout Korea as it is a must-try! I suggest using pre-cut coleslaw mix to save on time, but feel free to use any pre-chopped cabbage or carrot matchsticks. And, if you don't want to make it so spicy, just reduce the amount of gochugaru.

Place the rice cakes in a large bowl and cover with room temperature water. Set aside.

In large bowl, whisk together all the ingredients for the chicken marinade, then place the chicken in it. Set aside and allow to infuse.

Place a large non-stick frying pan over a medium-high heat and drizzle in the vegetable oil. Add the coleslaw mix or shredded cabbage and carrot, onion, spring onions and sweet potato.

Drain the rice cakes and place on top of the vegetables. Add the marinated chicken (and all the marinade) to the centre of the pan. Once you hear sizzling, mix everything well. Cook, stirring often to make sure the bottom doesn't burn, until the sweet potatoes are cooked through and the rice cakes are soft, about 8–9 minutes. Stir in all but a small handful of the kkaennip. Sprinkle over the remainder and serve immediately.

닭불고기

SERVES 4

Prep time: 15 minutes
Total time: 30 minutes

300ml (1¼ cups) soy sauce
100g (3½oz) dark brown sugar
3 tbsp mirim
2 tbsp doenjang (fermented soya
 bean paste)
2 tbsp roasted sesame oil
2 tbsp grated ginger
6 garlic cloves, grated
pinch of sea or kosher salt
freshly ground black pepper
8 boneless skinless chicken thighs,
 cut into 1cm (½in) strips
vegetable or other neutral oil,
 for cooking

To Serve

'sexy' spring onions (scallions) (follow
 step 1 on page 50)

For any barbecue meat or seafood
 dishes, feel free to serve these
 sharing plates alongside any sides
 and banchan of your choice. The
 most traditional and loved being
 cabbage kimchi (see page 56), ssam
 leaves (see page 16), gim (see page
 13), short-grain white rice and
 Ssamjang (see page 194).

The Ultimate Barbecue Chicken

Dak Bulgogi

Korea is best known for its barbecue – umami-filled addictive marinades and sauces infused into thin strips of meat. The sweet smoke alone will lure you to the table. Serve this chicken version with ssamjang sauce, rice and ssam (leafy greens). You can marinate the chicken in the fridge overnight, but not longer, as the soy sauce will start to cure the meat. Serve with Korean makgeolli (fermented rice drink) to wash it all down.

In a medium bowl, stir together the soy sauce, brown sugar, mirim, doenjang, sesame oil, ginger, garlic, salt and a generous amount of pepper. Whisk until the sugar has completely dissolved. Place the chicken in a resealable plastic freezer bag (preferably reusable) and pour the marinade on top. Close the bag tightly and massage the marinade into the chicken gently. Place in a shallow, wide bowl and allow to further marinate at room temperature for about 10 minutes. Set aside.

Meanwhile, place a large non-stick frying pan or griddle pan over a medium-high heat and drizzle generously with vegetable oil. Shake any excess marinade off the chicken and place the strips into the pan. Discard the marinade. Cook for 15 minutes, flipping often, until the chicken is cooked through and sticky. Transfer the chicken to a platter and sprinkle over the spring onions. Serve with the sides and banchan of your choice.

닭강정

SERVES 4

Prep time: 15 minutes
Total time: 30 minutes

900g (2lbs) boneless skin-on chicken
   thighs (or skinless), cut into 2.5cm
   (1in) pieces
125g (¾ cup) potato starch
1.5–2.6l (8–11 cups) vegetable or
   other neutral oil

For the Batter Mix

90g (½ cup) potato starch
30g (¼ cup) plain (all-purpose) flour
2½ tsp onion powder
2½ tsp garlic powder
½ tsp baking powder
1 tbsp sea or kosher salt

For the Spicy Chicken Sauce

2 tbsp gochujang (Korean chilli paste)
2 tbsp Korean rice syrup (or runny
   honey, to taste)
65ml (¼ cup) soy sauce
2 tbsp light brown sugar
1 tbsp rice vinegar
1 tbsp grated garlic
1 tbsp roasted sesame oil

To Serve

1 spring onion (scallion), thinly sliced
1 red chilli, preferably Korean but a
   Fresno will also work, thinly sliced
   (optional)

The Crispiest Korean Fried Chicken Bites

Dak Gangjeong

KFC, or Korean Fried Chicken, has become a global sensation! This simplified recipe skips the brining process, making it perfect for dark meat like thighs. However, it's also adaptable for wings or white meat – just be cautious not to overcook. To save time, ask your butcher to debone the chicken pieces for you. The secret to KFC's fame lies in this wet batter, delivering that iconic thin, crispy crust. And don't forget to generously coat these golden nuggets in the spicy chicken sauce!

Place a wire rack on a baking sheet. Dust the chicken pieces with the potato starch, shaking the excess off well. Place the chicken on the rack to dry out.

Next, make the batter mix. In a large bowl, whisk together all the ingredients. Set aside.

Now, make the spicy chicken sauce. Place a small saucepan over a medium-low heat. Add all the ingredients and whisk with 1 tbsp water. Bring up to a simmer and simmer for 3 minutes, then remove from the heat and set aside. Taste and adjust the seasoning.

In a large, wide, heavy-based saucepan at least 13cm (5in) deep, heat 5cm (2in) vegetable oil over a medium-high heat until it reaches 205°C (400°F). Place another wire rack over a baking sheet and put it next to the saucepan.

To the dry batter mix, add about 200ml (scant 1 cup) cold water and whisk together – the consistency of the batter should be like paint.

Using tongs, dip the chicken pieces one by one into the wet batter mix and fry for 2–3 minutes until they are golden brown and register 75°C (165°F) with a temperature probe. You'll have to hold each piece of chicken in the hot oil for a few seconds before releasing to prevent them sticking to the bottom. Fry as many pieces of chicken as can fit in the fryer without touching or crowding. Do not let the oil temperature dip below 180°C (350°F) to ensure crispiness. Place the cooked chicken on the clean rack.

Serve with the sauce on the side or drizzled over the top, or toss the chicken with the sauce. Garnish with spring onions and slices of chilli (if using), and serve immediately.

치즈불닭

Prep time: 15 minutes
Total time: 30 minutes

170g (1½ cups) tteok (Korean rice cakes), sliced

25g (¼ cup) gochugaru (Korean chilli flakes)

70g (¼ cup) gochujang (Korean chilli paste)

2 tbsp soy sauce

150g (¾ cup) dark brown sugar

2 tbsp roasted sesame oil

8 garlic cloves, grated

3 tsp grated ginger

2 tsp freshly ground black pepper

1 chicken stock (bouillon) cube, dissolved in 1 tbsp hot water

900g (2lbs) boneless skinless chicken thighs, trimmed of excess fat and cut into 2.5cm (1in) cubes

60ml (¼ cup) vegetable or other neutral oil

450g (4 cups) grated (shredded) low-moisture mozzarella (if not using grated cheese, dice the cheese into 1cm/½in pieces)

To Serve

1 spring onion (scallion), thinly sliced
roasted sesame seeds
steamed short-grain white rice

Spicy Fire Chicken with Cheese

'Chijeu' or Cheese Buldak

Buldak means 'fire chicken' and this recipe lives up to its name, with intense heat and bold flavours. I love the different textures in this red-hot dish – meaty and juicy chicken, chewy and toothsome rice cakes, and then ooey gooey cheese on top. It is the perfect casual party dish to share with friends.

Place the rice cakes in a large bowl and cover with room temperature water. Set aside.

In a large bowl, combine the gochugaru, gochujang, soy sauce, sugar, sesame oil, garlic, ginger, pepper and stock, and mix well. Add the chicken and mix well to coat.

Preheat the grill (broiler) of the oven to high.

In a large heavy-based ovenproof frying pan, drizzle in the oil and place over a medium-high heat. Tip in the chicken and all the gochujang mixture. Cook for about 5 minutes, stirring often. Drain and add the rice cakes then mix through and cook for a further 5 minutes until the rice cakes, are softened. Turn off the heat and sprinkle in the cheese. Place the pan under the grill (broiler) on high for about 5 minutes until the cheese is melted and slightly browned.

Garnish with spring onions and a sprinkle of sesame seeds. Serve with steamed short-grain rice.

RED

—MEAT

소불고기

SERVES 2–4

Prep time: 15 minutes
Total time: 30 minutes

450g (1lb) bulgogi beef (Korean-style
  very thinly sliced meat) or a ribeye
  or sirloin steak (or other prime cut
  of beef), trimmed
60ml (¼ cup) soy sauce
1 small Asian pear, or Conference or
  Bosc pear, peeled and cored
2 tsp grated garlic
2.5cm (1in) piece of ginger, roughly
  chopped
1 tbsp roasted sesame oil
1 tbsp light brown sugar
1 tbsp sake or pure soju
1 tbsp fish sauce or anchovy sauce
1½ tbsp mirim
1 brown (yellow) onion, thinly sliced
freshly ground black pepper

To Serve

5 chives, thinly sliced
1 tsp roasted sesame seeds
steamed short-grain white rice
  (optional)
kimchi (optional)
ssam (leafy greens) (optional)

The Best Bulgogi Beef

So Bulgogi

Bulgogi is one of Korea's most-loved dishes. I like to cook this classic dish in a frying pan to savour the juices. Be sure to spoon these delicious juices over your rice. Serve with a bit of kimchi on the side and dinner is sorted. Thinly sliced bulgogi meat is available at most Asian supermarkets. I have made this recipe time and time again, and it never disappoints!

If using steaks, put in the freezer for about 2 hours until partially frozen. Remove from the freezer and use a sharp knife to cut the meat into slices about 5mm (¼in) thick.

In a food processor, combine the soy sauce, pear, garlic, ginger, sesame oil, sugar, sake, fish sauce or anchovy sauce, mirim and a little pepper. Blend until smooth.

Place the beef in a resealable plastic freezer bag (preferably reusable). Pour the marinade into the freezer bag with the meat and add the onion. Close the bag tightly and gently massage the marinade into the meat.

Heat a griddle pan or frying pan over a high heat. Alternatively, heat a charcoal grill and place a speciality bulgogi griddle pan over it. Once hot, cook the bulgogi in batches with the marinade, flipping often, until desired doneness is reached, about 2 minutes.

Remove from the heat and place on a serving platter. Pour any juices from the pan over the meat. Garnish with chopped chives and sesame seeds. Serve with rice, kimchi and ssam, or whatever you like!

육회

Korean Steak
Tartare

Yukhoe

SERVES 2–4

Prep time: 25 minutes
Total time: 25 minutes

1 small Asian pear, or Conference
   or Bosc pear, peeled, cored and
   julienned
285g (10oz) beef fillet (filet mignon),
   trimmed and partially frozen (about
   30 minutes
   in the freezer)
1 tbsp lemon juice
3 chives, thinly sliced on a bias
1 tsp grated garlic
2 tbsp soy sauce
2 tsp runny honey
1 tsp roasted sesame seeds
2 tbsp roasted sesame oil
2 tbsp finely chopped shallots
2 tbsp pine nuts, toasted
flaked sea or kosher salt
freshly ground black pepper

<u>To Serve</u>

4 quail egg yolks in half shells
   (optional)
freshly ground black pepper
bugak (seaweed tempura chips)
   (optional)

I am always surprised that Korean steak tartare is not more well known. It boasts a very different flavour profile from its famed French counterpart. Korea's version proves lighter, boasting crisp, fresh pear, nutty sesame oil and roasted pine nuts. It's perfect to serve as a starter or even as canapés on toast.

Place the pear in a small bowl of cold water with the lemon juice to prevent it from turning brown. Let sit for 5–10 minutes and then drain well.

With a sharp knife, cut the beef into skinny batons about 5mm (¼in) thick and 5cm (2in) long. Place in a bowl.

In a separate medium bowl, whisk together the chives, garlic, soy sauce, honey, sesame seeds, sesame oil, shallots, pine nuts and salt and pepper to taste. Add more honey, if you prefer it a bit sweeter. Pour over the beef strips and mix well.

To serve, mound the tartare in the centre of your plates, then serve the pear alongside or around the beef. Make a small well in each mound of beef and put a quail yolk in each (if using). Garnish with a few grinds of pepper. Serve immediately, with bugak (if using).

양념갈비

양념갈비

My Most-loved Marinated Beef Short Ribs

Yangnyeom Galbi

SERVES 2

Active time: 30 minutes
Total time: 2 hours, plus marinating

1 small Asian pear, or 2 firm but ripe
  Conference pears, peeled, cored
  and roughly chopped
260ml (1 cup) mirim
2 tbsp dark brown sugar
3 tbsp soy sauce
2½ tbsp roasted sesame oil
3 garlic cloves, peeled
½ brown (yellow) onion, thinly sliced
2.5cm (1in) piece ginger, grated
large pinch of flaked sea or kosher
  salt
1 tsp freshly ground black pepper
450g (1lb) bone-in beef short ribs (or
  trimmed boneless ribeye steak,
  partially frozen and cut into
  5mm/¼in thick pieces)
vegetable or other neutral oil,
  for cooking

To Serve

Sides and banchan of your choice
  (see page 78)

Everyone knows this traditional Korean barbecue dish. Short ribs are the cut of choice, with great marbling and meaty flavour. The marinade is what makes this dish memorable – full of classic Korean aromatics and deep, rich umami notes. Korean barbecue beef and Appa's Ice-cold Noodles (see page 74) is a classic pairing and you'll often be served a bowl of these ice-cold noodles after polishing off your galbi.

Put the pear, mirim, brown sugar, soy sauce, sesame oil, garlic, onion, ginger, salt and pepper into a blender and blend until smooth. Place the short ribs into a large resealable freezer bag (preferable reusable), and pour the marinade over. Seal the bag tightly and massage the meat gently. Place the bag in a bowl set aside in the refridgerator to marinate. The longer you marinate the beef, the better it will taste.

Place a griddle pan over a high heat or prepare a gas or charcoal barbecue (grill) and heat until very hot. Once the griddle or barbecue is very hot, lightly brush it with vegetable oil.

Using tongs, place the beef on the griddle or barbecue, shaking off any excess marinade. Cook for 20–30 seconds per side for rare, or longer to your desired doneness. Transfer the meat to a platter and serve with the sides and banchan of your choice.

소시지 김치전

MAKES 2 X 20CM (8IN)
PANCAKES

Prep time: 12 minutes
Total time: 30 minutes

90g (¾ cup) buchim garu (Korean
  pancake mix)
90g (¾ cup) twigim garu (Korean
  frying mix)
225g (1½ cup) ripe cabbage kimchi,
  drained and finely chopped
60ml (¼ cup) ripe kimchi juice
2 spring onions (scallions), split
  lengthwise and cut into 2.5cm
  (1in) slices
2 pinches of sea or kosher salt
vegetable or other neutral oil,
  for frying
180g (6oz) plain pork sausages (or
  sausages of your choice), casing
  removed, or loose sausage meat

To Serve
Jeon Dipping Sauce (see page 195)

Truly Delectable Kimchi & Pork Sausage Pancakes

Sosiji Kimchi Jeon

I have cooked these pancakes on many morning shows – such a crowd-pleaser! I like to use sausage meat as it adds a bit more flavour, but feel free to use minced (ground) or any cut of fresh pork you like. Do choose a relatively plain-flavoured sausage, though, as any potent herbs or spices may overpower the kimchi flavour.

In a medium bowl, stir together the buchim garu, twigim garu, kimchi, kimchi juice, spring onions, salt and 175ml (¾ cup) water until just combined into a lumpy batter. Do not overmix.

In a 20cm (8in) wide non-stick frying pan, heat 1 tbsp of oil over a medium-high heat and add the sausage. Break it up into small pieces and cook for about 4 minutes until brown. Drain off the excess oil, add the sausage to the batter and mix until combined.

Add 3–4 tbsp more oil to the pan and pour half of the batter. Cook until golden brown on the base, 3–4 minutes. Flip the pancake and press down firmly with the back of a non-stick spatula. Add in 2–3 tbsp more oil around the edges of the pancake and continue cooking until the other side is golden brown, about 3 minutes more, making sure to gently and firmly press the pancake down. Transfer to a wire rack or paper towel-lined plate to soak up the excess oil. Repeat with the remaining batter, adding more oil as needed. Transfer to a platter and serve immediately with the dipping sauce.

버섯고기만두

MAKES 25 DUMPLINGS

Prep time: 12 minutes
Total time: 30 minutes

For the Filling

170g (6oz) minced (ground) pork or
   beef (or a mixture of the two)
45g (3oz) shiitake or oyster
   mushrooms, finely chopped
70g (2½oz) finely shredded baechu
   (Chinese leaf/Napa cabbage), ribs
   removed
1 spring onion (scallion), thinly sliced
½ tbsp soy sauce
½ tbsp roasted sesame oil
1 large garlic clove, grated
½ tsp sea or kosher salt
½ tsp grated ginger
½ tsp roasted sesame seeds
½ tsp caster (superfine) sugar
freshly ground black pepper

For the Dumplings

25 thin, round, eggless dumpling
   wrappers
vegetable or other neutral oil,
   for frying

To Serve

Jeon Dipping Sauce (see page 195)

Tip

You can freeze the dumplings for up
to 3 months. To cook from frozen,
place 1 tbsp vegetable oil in a large
non-stick frying pan or wok over a
medium-high heat. Add the
dumplings and fry for 1–2 minutes,
then add 2 tbsp of water and reduce
the heat to low. Cover with a lid and
steam for 5–6 minutes.

Umma's Meat & Mushroom Dumplings

Beoseot Gogi Mandu

My sister and I used to help our mom to make hundreds of mandu (dumplings) when we were young. We would sit at the kitchen table for hours folding and shaping these chubby parcels. My mom would cook them in a variety of ways: boiled, steamed or pan-fried. But pan-fried mandu were my favourite, as the dumpling wrappers would soak up all the meat's juices and fat and become lip-smackingly crispy. I would rip off these flavourful skins and snack on them, tossing the meaty interior to my sister to enjoy. I still think the fried wrappers are the best part...

In a large bowl, combine all the filling ingredients and mix together using your hands until fully incorporated. Fry off a small patty in a non-stick frying pan until cooked through and taste to check the seasoning. Add more salt or pepper to taste and mix well.

Line a baking sheet with baking parchment and set aside. Fill a small bowl with water. Unwrap the dumpling wrappers and cover lightly with a piece of cling film (plastic wrap) to keep them from drying out. Fill each wrapper with 1 tbsp of the filling. Dip a finger into the water and wet the edges of the wrapper. Fold the wrapper in half and press the edges firmly together to seal, pressing out any air bubbles. You can also crimp the edges to make a frill, as pictured. Line the dumplings up on the prepared baking sheet. Repeat with the remaining wrappers and filling, making sure the dumplings aren't touching on the baking sheet. Once the dumplings are assembled, if you don't plan to cook them straightaway you can freeze them on the baking sheet, then bag them up to store in the freezer.

To pan-fry the dumplings, heat a large non-stick frying pan over a medium-high heat and add 1 tbsp oil. Working in batches, lay the dumplings on their sides in the pan in a single layer without crowding the pan. Cook for 2–3 minutes until golden brown on the base. Flip them and cook for a further 2–3 minutes until golden brown and the filling is cooked through. Transfer the fried dumplings to a wire rack or paper towel-lined plate to drain. Repeat with the remaining dumplings, adding more oil to the pan as needed.

If you prefer not to fry the dumplings, steam them in batches until cooked through, about 5–6 minutes, then transfer to a serving platter.

Transfer the fried dumplings to a platter and serve immediately, with the dipping sauce.

삼겹살 구이

SERVES 4

Prep time: 12 minutes
Total time: 30 minutes

4 garlic cloves
4 tbsp roasted sesame oil
vegetable or other neutral oil,
  for frying
1.3kg (3lbs) pork belly, skin removed,
  very thinly sliced (see tip) and cut
  into 7.5cm (3in) wide pieces
1 large brown (yellow) onion, sliced
  into 1cm (½in) thick rings,

To Serve
Sides and banchan of your choice
  (see page 78)

Tip
For ease, you can buy pork belly cut
into 1mm slices in an Asian
supermarket. Alternatively freeze the
pork belly for two hours, then slice it
as thinly as possible (5mm/¼in
should be the maximum thickness
but go thinner, if possible).

Perfect Pork Belly Barbecue

Samgyeopsal Gui

I have so many great memories of eating samgyeopsal in Seoul. Whole streets are closed down and filled with specially made tables with barbecue grills built right into them. You can smell the sweet smoke from blocks away, enticing you to grab a seat and start grilling.

Cut a square of foil about 15 x 15cm (6 x 6in) and place the garlic in the centre. Bring the sides of the foil up to make a cup and pour in the sesame oil. Close up the foil to create a small parcel.

Heat a large non-stick frying pan over a medium-high heat and drizzle with a bit of vegetable oil. Place the garlic parcel on one side of the pan, then add enough of the pork belly to cover the bottom of the frying pan in one layer. Cook until the edges of the pork belly are browned and crispy, about 6–7 minutes depending on thickness. Place on a plate lined with paper towels and repeat until all the pork is cooked, draining the fat from the pan as necessary.

Place the onion rings in the frying pan and cook until browned on the edges and just translucent. Put on the plate with the pork belly. Carefully remove the garlic parcel from the pan, allow to cool slightly. The garlic should be soft. Tip into a small dish.

Place the pork and onions on a serving platter and serve with the sides and banchan of your choice.

두부김치

SERVES 4

Prep time: 10 minutes
Total time: 25 minutes

450g (1lb) firm tofu, drained
350g (2 cups) ripe cabbage kimchi
  and juice, cut into 5cm (2in) pieces
350g (12oz) pork tenderloin, shoulder
  or belly, very thinly sliced (see tip
  on page 96) and cut into 5cm (2in)
  wide pieces
1 tbsp soy sauce
1 tbsp grated garlic
1 tbsp grated ginger
2 tsp caster (superfine) sugar
2 spring onions (scallions), halved
  lengthwise, then cut into 5cm
  (2in) pieces
1 tbsp roasted sesame oil
1 tsp roasted sesame seeds
freshly ground black pepper
2 tbsp vegetable or other neutral oil

To Serve

1 spring onion (scallion), thinly sliced
  on a bias
black and white roasted sesame
  seeds

My Go-to Stir-fried Pork, Kimchi & Tofu

Dubukimchi

This simple dish showcases three of my most loved ingredients: kimchi, pork and tofu! And, better yet, it is ready on the table in no time. If you cannot find thin (shabu shabu style) pork, then partially freeze pork tenderloin, belly, or shoulder, and thinly slice it with a sharp knife.

Make sure the kimchi is very ripe... the riper the better!

Place a foldable steamer or steamer basket inside a medium lidded saucepan and add water to the pan until it just touches the bottom of the steamer. Cut the tofu block in half, place it into the steamer basket and place the pan over a high heat. Cover and bring to the boil. Cook for 4–5 minutes until hot and warmed through entirely. Remove from the heat but keep the lid on to keep the tofu warm. Alternatively, place the tofu in a large heatproof bowl with 2 tbsp of water. Cover with a heatproof plate and microwave on high for 5 minutes. Leave covered until ready to slice.

In a large bowl, mix together the kimchi, pork, soy sauce, garlic, ginger, sugar, spring onions, sesame oil, sesame seeds and pepper to taste. Mix well to coat the pork and set aside.

Place a large non-stick frying pan over a medium-high heat and drizzle with the oil. Add the pork kimchi mixture and sauté until the pork is cooked through and the kimchi is softened and dried out a bit, about 9–10 minutes. Remove from the heat.

Carefully remove the warm tofu from the steamer, or the bowl if microwaved, put on a cutting board and pat with paper towels to remove excess moisture. Cut the tofu in half again, lengthwise, and then evenly slice into triangles about 1.5cm (¾in) thick.

Dip some of the triangles into the black and white sesame seeds, so that they coat one side. These look particularly striking when some are coated in white seeds, some in black and the remainder in both seeds mixed together.

Scoop the kimchi pork stir-fry into the middle of a plate. Place the tofu next to the stir-fry. Garnish with sliced spring onions and serve immediately.

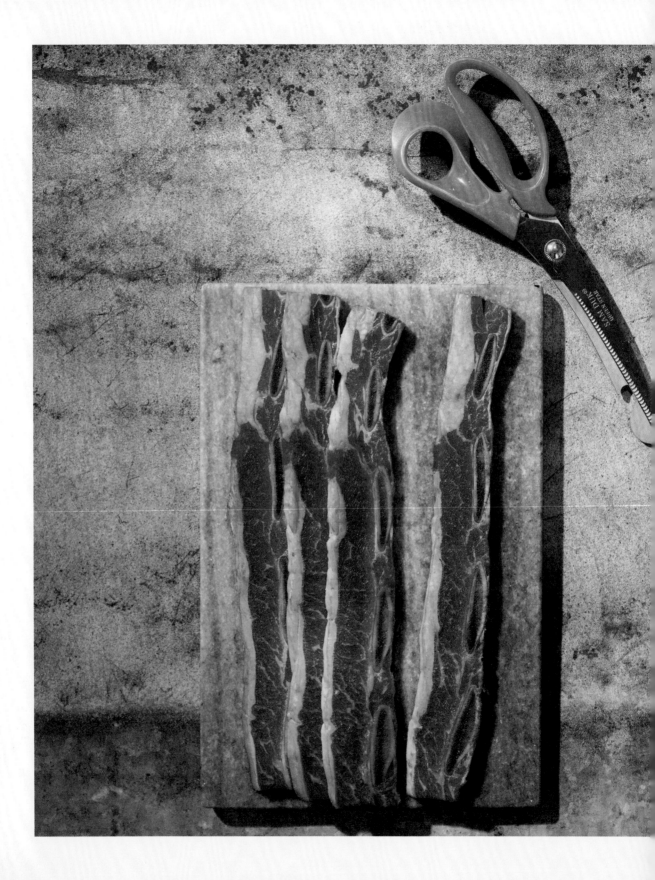

SEAFOOD

고등어 구이

The Simplest Grilled or Pan-fried Mackerel

Godeungeo Gui

SERVES 4

Prep time: 22 minutes
Total time: 30 minutes

4 x 150g (5½oz) boneless mackerel
  fillets, halved crosswise, patted dry
vegetable or other neutral oil, for
  cooking
30g (¼ cup) plain (all-purpose) flour, if
  pan-frying
sea or kosher salt
freshly ground black pepper

To Serve

4–5 chopped chives, cut into 2cm
  (1in) pieces
steamed short-grain white rice
cabbage kimchi (see page 56)
1 lemon, deseeded and cut into
  wedges

My mom used to make this mega-easy grilled mackerel in our worn-out little toaster oven as an afternoon snack. I used to wait anxiously, listening to the soft ticking timer, counting down the minutes before it was done, which was announced by a loud, hollow 'ding!' She would lay the fish on a bed of rice and splash a bit of soy sauce or ponzu on top. On the side, I would have small pieces of kimchi that she'd wash in water and cut up for me, a non-spicy version for kids. I still love eating this meal today, but I don't wash the kimchi off.

For grilled mackerel, preheat the grill (broiler), or a toaster oven with grill function, and position a wire rack below it. Line a baking sheet with foil and oil the foil. Lightly coat both sides of the mackerel with oil, season with salt and pepper generously and arrange skin-side down on the prepared baking sheet. Grill until the fish is lightly golden and the flesh is cooked through, about 5 minutes.

For pan-fried mackerel, season both sides of the fish with salt and pepper. Pour the flour out on a large plate and coat both sides of the fillets in flour. Tap off the excess, then place the fish on a clean plate. Drizzle a non-stick frying pan generously with oil and place over a high heat. Once the oil is hot, place the fish in the pan and cook skin-side down for 3–4 minutes, then flip and cook for an additional 3–4 minutes, depending on how thick the fillets are. Once done, place the cooked pieces of fish on a plate lined with paper towels to soak up any excess oil.

Garnish the mackerel with chives and serve with rice, kimchi and lemon wedges.

Tip

Feel free to use frozen or fresh mackerel. Just be sure to thaw the frozen fish completely before cooking.

고추장 연어스테이크

SERVES 4

Prep time: 8 minutes
Total time: 20 minutes

vegetable or other neutral oil,
  for greasing
4 x 100g (3½oz) boneless skin-on
  salmon fillets

For the Gochujang Glaze

1⅓ tbsp gochujang (Korean chilli
  paste)
1 tbsp thinly sliced spring onions
  (scallions)
1 heaped tbsp caster (superfine)
  sugar
½ tsp grated garlic
2 tsp grated ginger

To Serve

steamed multi-grain rice
Spinach Banchan (see page 24)
spring onions (scallions), thinly sliced

Sweet & Spicy Gochujang Salmon

Gochujang Yeoneo Seuteikeu

The rich, oily flavour of salmon pairs so well with the spicy-sweet fruity notes of gochujang. Feel free to slather this versatile glaze on cod, halibut or snapper too. And, do spoon any extra glaze from the pan on your rice... it's oh so good.

Preheat the oven to 160°C fan/180°C/350°F/gas 4 and line a baking sheet with foil. Grease the foil with a bit of oil.

For the gochujang glaze, whisk together the gochujang, spring onion, sugar, garlic and ginger in a small bowl.

Lay the salmon skin-side down on the prepared baking sheet, spread the glaze on top of the salmon and let marinate while the oven comes to temperature.

Cook on the middle shelf of the oven for 10–12 minutes until cooked to the desired doneness.

To serve, spread the rice out over a large platter, leaving space on one side. Spoon the spinach banchan into the space. Place the salmon fillets on top of the rice and garnish with the spring onions.

생선전

SERVES 4

Prep time: 20 minutes
Total time: 30 minutes

450g (1lb) cod fillets, skin removed,
cut into 1cm (½in) thick pieces
sea or kosher salt
freshly ground black pepper
125g (¾ cup) potato starch
4 large eggs
60ml (¼ cup) vegetable or other
neutral oil

<u>To Serve</u>

1 spring onion (scallion), thinly sliced
on a bias
Jeon Dipping Sauce (see page 195)

Yuna's Battered & Pan-fried Fish

Saengseon Jeon

My little niece, Yuna, is addicted to these lightly pan-fried fish fillets. She smiles from ear to ear! My mom makes the best ones – always selecting the freshest fish and slicing it thinly, making for a truly delicate bite. You can sub out the cod and use butterflied prawns (shrimp), oysters, tofu and other types of white fish (whiting, flounder, hake or plaice).

Place the cod fillets on a plate and season well with salt and pepper on both sides.

On a large plate, tip out the potato starch. In a wide bowl, whisk the eggs with a pinch of salt.

Place a non-stick frying pan over a medium-low heat and drizzle generously with oil. Dry off the fish, dredge lightly through the potato starch and shake off the excess, then place on a clean plate. The flour should be a thin dusting on the fish. Next, dip the fillets in the egg, allowing the excess to drip off. Place the coated fish immediately in the frying pan. Repeat until the pan is full.

Cook the fish slowly, flipping as necessary, trying not to allow the egg to brown too much (keep the colour of the egg as yellow as possible), about 1 minute on each side. Once done, place the cooked fish on a plate lined with paper towels. Repeat until all the fish is cooked. Scatter the spring onion on top to finish and serve with the dipping sauce.

고등어 구이

SERVES 2–4

Prep time: 17 minutes
Total time: 25 minutes

450g (1lb) jumbo king prawns
(shrimp), peeled, tail-on and
deveined

For the Marinade

2 tbsp vegetable or other neutral oil,
plus extra for grilling
1 tbsp grated garlic
1 tsp grated ginger
½ brown (yellow) onion, very thinly
sliced
2 tbsp gochujang (Korean chilli paste)
1½ tbsp doenjang (fermented soya
bean paste)
1 tbsp mirim
2 tsp fish sauce
2 tsp caster (superfine) sugar
freshly ground black pepper

To Serve

2 tsp roasted sesame oil
1 tsp chopped chives
1 red chilli, preferably Korean but a
Fresno will also work, thinly sliced
Sides and banchan of your choice
(see page 78)

Epic Barbecue Prawns

Yangnyeom Saewoo Gui

I am a huge seafood fan, and this easy barbecue prawn (shrimp) recipe will surely impress your guests. Tail-on jumbo king prawns always look luxurious, and when doused in an aromatic garlicky sauce, they will taste exquisite too. My dad absolutely loves this sweet and spicy marinade, which compliments the subtle sweetness of the prawns. They are a great option to serve alongside short ribs (see page 90) for a 'surf and turf' Korean barbecue.

In a medium-sized bowl, mix together all the marinade ingredients until well incorporated. Add the prawns and mix to coat well. Marinate for at least 5 minutes.

Meanwhile, heat a large cast-iron frying pan or griddle pan over a high heat. Once hot, brush lightly with oil. Using tongs, place the prawns in the pan. Cook for about 2 minutes, flipping as necessary and brushing generousy with extra marinade, until the prawns are nearly cooked through. Tip in the rest of the marinade, including the onions, and sauté with the prawns until the onions are caramelized.

Place the prawns on a plate, drizzle with sesame oil, then sprinkle over the chives and the red chilli slices. Serve with the sides and banchan of your choice.

해물파전

Umma Do's Seafood Pancakes

Haemul Pajeon

SERVES 4

Prep time: 14 minutes
Total time: 30 minutes

95g (¾ cup) buchim garu (Korean
    pancake mix)
95g (¾ cup) twigim garu (Korean
    frying mix)
140g (1 cup) frozen seafood mix
    (variety of mussels, squid, prawns/
    shrimp, imitation crab sticks, etc.),
    rinsed with cold water and chopped
    into 1cm (½in) pieces
6 spring onions (scallions), trimmed,
    split lengthwise and sliced into 2cm
    (1in) pieces
15g (½oz) thinly sliced red chillis,
    preferably Korean but Fresnos will
    also work
vegetable or other neutral oil,
    for frying

To Serve
Umma Do's Chojang (see page 190)
chopped chives (optional)

Seafood pancakes are one of Korea's most popular dishes. My recipe tester Jessica Do's umma (mom) makes these pancakes often and employs a well-known trick among Korean cooks – use shop-bought pancake mix combined with frying mix. Umma Do says that the perfect ratio is 1:1 buchim garu to twigim garu, which makes perfectly crispy pancakes every time. She would also make a large batch of the batter mix in the morning and store it in the fridge to fry later that evening. It gets better as it sits. Don't turn your nose up at the pre-packaged pancake or frying mix... all Korean ummas swear by it. I do too!

In a large bowl, combine the buchim garu, twigim garu and 235ml (1 cup) cold water, then mix with chopsticks until just combined and lumpy. Do not overmix. Add the frozen seafood mix, spring onions and chillis. Stir the batter until just thoroughly combined.

In a 25–30cm (10–12in) non-stick frying pan, heat 3–4 tbsp of oil over a medium-high heat. When the oil is shimmering, add half the pancake batter and spread out into a 7.5cm (3in) wide circle. You should be able to fit three pancakes into the pan at once. Fry for 3–4 minutes until golden brown and crispy on the base and around the edges. Carefully flip and add another 1–2 tbsp of vegetable oil around the edges of the pancake, then gently and firmly press down the pancake with a non-stick spatula and cook for a further 3–4 minutes until the other side is golden. Transfer to a plate lined with paper towels to soak up the excess oil or a wire rack placed over a baking sheet. Repeat with the remaining batter, adding more oil to the frying pan as needed. Serve immediately, with the dipping sauce, and garnish with chives, if you like.

오지어볶음

___

SERVES 4

Prep time: 15 minutes
Total time: 30 minutes

2 tbsp grated garlic
3 tbsp gochujang (Korean chilli paste)
2 tbsp fish sauce
1 tbsp roasted sesame oil
1½ tbsp light brown sugar
450g (1lb) frozen or fresh squid rings
  or slices
1 tbsp vegetable or other neutral oil
2 small carrots (about 100g/3½oz),
  peeled and thinly sliced
1 red onion, thinly sliced
8 spring onions (scallions), green
  parts only, or ½ bunch of Chinese
  chives, cut into 4cm (1½in) pieces

To Serve

steamed short-grain white or
  black rice
silgochu (chilli threads)

Fiery Squid Stir-fry

Ojingeo Bokkeum

My dad loves this fiery squid stir-fry. I like to use fresh squid, as it comes out more tender, but frozen squid is very good too. Feel free to add any vegetables of your choice, such as colourful (bell) peppers. Definitely serve this dish with rice to soak up the delicious sauce.

In a medium bowl, stir together the garlic, gochujang, fish sauce, sesame oil and sugar until the sugar is fully dissolved. Set aside. Add the squid to the sauce and toss to coat. Leave to marinate at room temperature for 10 minutes.

In a large frying pan, heat the vegetable oil over a medium-high heat. Add the carrots and red onion and cook for about 2 minutes, stirring frequently, until the carrots have softened, but are still firm. Add the squid and sauce and cook for 2–3 minutes, stirring frequently, until the squid is firm but tender and just cooked through. Do not overcook or the squid will become tough. Stir in the spring onion greens or chives and remove from the heat.

To serve, spread the rice on a plate and spoon over the squid and sauce. Top with silgochu and enjoy.

Tip

Feel free to use frozen squid. There's no need to thaw it before using, just add it straight to the marinade.

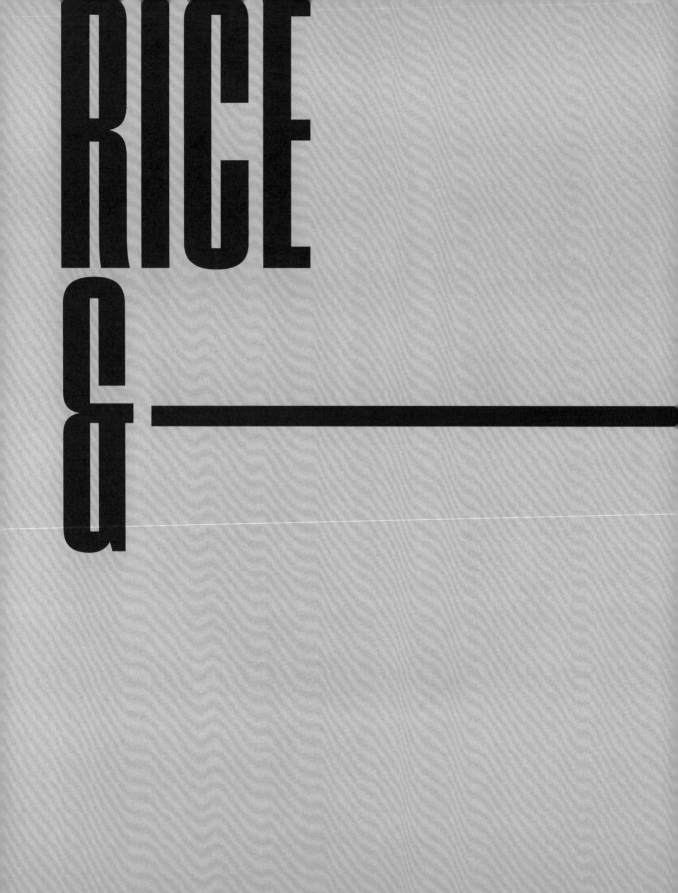

— NOODLES

떡볶이

SERVES 4–6

Prep time: 20 minutes
Total time: 30 minutes

200g (7oz) eomuk (fish cake sheets),
  cut into triangular pieces about
  7.5cm (3in) long (for a vegetarian
  alternative, use 120g/4oz dried
  bean-curd sticks or bean-curd
  sheets)
450g (1lb) gaerae-tteok (cylindrical
  rice cakes), 5cm (2in) long
1l (4 cups) Anchovy Dashi Stock (see
  page 192) or Vegetable Dashi Stock
  (see page 193), or 1 tbsp anchovy
  dashida (Korean anchovy stock
  powder) dissolved in 1l
  (4 cups) water
270g (9½oz) baechu (Chinese leaf/
  Napa cabbage), chopped
2 carrots, peeled and thinly sliced on
  a bias
1 brown (yellow) onion, thinly sliced
2 garlic cloves, grated
210g (¾ cup) gochujang (Korean chilli
  paste)
2 tbsp caster (superfine) sugar
1 tbsp soy sauce
1 tbsp gochugaru (Korean chilli
  flakes)

To Serve
2–3 large eggs, hard-boiled, peeled
  and quartered lengthwise
2 spring onions (scallions) thinly
  sliced on a bias

Spicy Rice Cakes & Fish Cakes

Tteokbokki

I have so many awesome memories of eating this spicy rice cake dish on the streets of Seoul after a late night clubbing! Chopsticks were hardly ever given out, only toothpicks, so we had to skewer these chewy rice cakes with great skill to avoid dropping them. To make a vegetarian version, use bean curd sheets, which have a similar texture to fish cakes, but are slightly chewier.

If you're making the vegetarian option, put the bean curd sticks or sheets in a bowl and pour over just enough boiling water to cover them. Once rehydrated, drain and cut into 7.5cm (3in) pieces. Set aside.

Place the gaerae-tteok in a large bowl and cover with warm water. Set aside.

In a large, wide, deep-frying pan, pour in the stock and bring it to a simmer. Add the cabbage, carrots, onion, garlic, gochujang, sugar, soy sauce and gochugaru, stir to combine well and simmer for 5 minutes. Drain the gaerae-tteok, then add them along with the eomuk (or the rehydrated bean curd) and cook, stirring occasionally, for about 5 minutes until the sauce has thickened slightly and the gaerae-tteok are softened. Nestle the eggs in the sauce, top with the spring onions, and serve immediately.

궁중떡볶이

SERVES 4

Prep time: 20 minutes
Total time: 30 minutes

For the Stir-fry

280g (10oz) tteok (Korean rice cakes),
   no thicker than 1.5cm (¾in) and no
   longer than 7cm (3in)
vegetable or other neutral oil,
   for frying
1 red onion, sliced about 5mm
   (¼in) thick
120g (4oz) shiitake mushrooms,
   sliced about 1cm (½in) thick
1 carrot, peeled, halved lengthwise
   and thinly sliced on a bias
½ courgette (zucchini) (preferably
   a Korean courgette or aehobak),
   sliced into batons about 5mm
   (¼in) thick

For the Beef and Marinade

450g (1lb) beef ribeye, trimmed and
   thinly sliced about 5mm (¼in) thick,
   or beef bulgogi (Korean-style very
   thinly sliced meat)
2 tbsp light brown sugar
1 tbsp mirim
60ml (¼ cup) soy sauce
2 tbsp roasted sesame oil
1 tbsp vegetable or other neutral oil
1 tbsp grated garlic
1 tbsp roasted sesame seeds,
   crushed
½ tsp freshly ground black pepper

To Serve

1 spring onion (scallion), sliced thinly
   on a bias
1 quail egg, soft-boiled and halved
black sesame seeds

Truly Royal Tteokbokki

Gungjung Tteokbokki

My father makes versions of this recipe occasionally when he feels brave enough to venture into the kitchen. He is a serious tteok fan, and this dish is no exception. You can use fresh tteok, just don't soak it, and cook it less, about 3–4 minutes. You can also use different-shaped tteok, like joraengi tteok (twin pearl-shaped, as pictured) or small thin garae-tteok (cylinder-shaped).

First, in a medium bowl, place the tteok in enough warm water to cover. Set aside and leave to soak while you make the rest of the recipe.

Next, make the beef marinade. In a shallow dish, combine the beef, brown sugar, mirim, soy sauce, sesame oil, vegetable oil, garlic, sesame seeds and black pepper and massage with your hands to thoroughly combine. Leave to marinate at room temperature.

For the stir-fry, heat a drizzle of vegetable oil in a large non-stick frying pan over a medium-high heat. Add the onion, mushrooms, carrot and courgette and cook for 3 minutes until slightly softened. Increase the heat to high, then add the beef with all the marinade. Drain the tteok, reserving the water, and add the tteok to the pan with about 4 tbsp of the soaking water. Cook for 6–7 minutes, stirring occasionally, until the sauce is thickened and begins to coat the beef. Transfer to a serving plate and arrange the spring onion and quail egg on top. Finish with a sprinkle of black sesame seeds.

Folded Kimbap

사각김밥

MAKES 2 FOLDED RICE 'SANDWICHES'

Sagak Kimbap

Kimbap has just gotten SO much easier to make! Think of this folded version like a seaweed sandwich, with endless filling possibilities. Feel free to use any leftover banchan to stuff inside, such as spinach, bean sprouts or aubergine (eggplant) (see pages 21–25). When getting ready to assemble the kimbap, make sure you have all of your ingredients prepared and close by. Lunch was never so easy!

Veggie: Danmuji, Yubu, Spinach & Carrots

Prep time: 23 minutes
Total time: 25 minutes

The yubu adds great texture and sweetness to this version.

For the Rice

200g (1 cup) steamed short-grain
  white rice
1 tbsp roasted sesame oil
1 tsp roasted sesame seeds
sea or kosher salt

For the Filling

1 tbsp vegetable or other neutral oil
30g (¼ cup) packaged grated
  (shredded) or julienned carrots
8 sheets of tinned seasoned yubu
  (tofu skin)
25g (1oz) baby spinach, washed and
  dried
12 thin slices of danmuji (yellow
  pickled radish)
sea or kosher salt

To Assemble

2 gim (roasted seaweed) sheets,
  about 19 x 22cm (7½ x 8½in)

Mix the rice with the sesame oil, sesame seeds and salt in a bowl. Set aside.

Heat a non-stick frying pan over a medium-high heat. Add the oil and the carrots and sauté for 2 minutes until the carrots are tender. Add salt to taste, remove from the heat, drain, and place the carrots in a bowl. Set aside.

Place a sheet of seaweed on a clean surface, shiny side down and longer side at the bottom. Fold in half, then in half again to quarter it (you should have a square). Unfold the seaweed and, using scissors, cut through one of the shorter folds between two squares, stopping at the centre point, then position that fold at the bottom. Wet your fingertips with water and spread half the rice evenly over the bottom right square, all the way to the edges.

Place half the yubu on the top right quadrant and half the danmuji on the top left square. Place some spinach leaves on the bottom left quadrant and top with half the carrots. Fold each quadrant up in a clockwise direction starting with the bottom left, to make a square wrap 'sandwich'. Repeat with the remaining ingredients.

Egg, Avocado & Cheese

Prep time: 17 minutes
Total time: 25 minutes

For the Rice

200g (1 cup) steamed short-grain
 white rice
1 tbsp roasted sesame oil
1 tsp roasted sesame seeds
sea or kosher salt

For the Filling

2 tbsp vegetable or other neutral oil
2 large eggs
½ avocado, cut into thin slices
2 cheese slices of your choice

To Assemble

2 gim (roasted seaweed) sheets,
 about 19 x 22cm (7½ x 8½in)

This version makes for a great breakfast sando on the go.

Mix the rice with the sesame oil, sesame seeds and salt in a bowl. Set aside.

Heat a non-stick pan frying over a medium heat and add half the vegetable oil. Add 1 egg and fry, breaking the yolk and gently forming it into a 7.5 x 7.5cm (3 x 3in) square. Repeat with the other egg and set aside.

Place a sheet of seaweed on a clean surface, shiny side down and longer side at the bottom. Fold in half, then in half again to quarter it (you should have a square). Unfold the seaweed and, using scissors, cut through one of the shorter folds between two squares, stopping at the centre point, then position that fold at the bottom. Wet your fingertips with water and spread half the rice evenly over the bottom right square, all the way to the edges.

Place a fried egg on the top left quadrant of seaweed and a slice of cheese on the top right, with half the avocado slices on the remaining quadrant. Fold each quadrant up in a clockwise direction, starting with the bottom left, to make a square wrap 'sandwich'. Repeat with the remaining ingredients.

Spam, Fried Egg & Kimchi

Prep time: 15 minutes
Total time: 25 minutes

For the Rice

200g (1 cup) steamed short-grain
 white rice
1 tbsp roasted sesame oil
1 tsp roasted sesame seeds
sea or kosher salt

For the Filling

4–6 slices of Spam (5mm/¼in thick)
2 large eggs
75g (¼ cup) cabbage kimchi (see
 page 56), chopped
2 kkaennip (perilla leaves) (optional)

To Assemble

2 gim (roasted seaweed) sheets,
 about 19 x 22cm (7½ x 8½in)

In Korea, Spam is a luxury item and truly coveted! I grew up eating this 'sort-of-possibly-almost meat', but feel free to substitute sausages or ham.

Mix the rice with the sesame oil, sesame seeds and salt in a bowl. Set aside.

Heat a non-stick frying pan over a medium-high heat. Fry the Spam until golden brown, then set aside on a paper towel-lined plate, leaving the Spam oil in the pan. Lower the heat to medium, then add 1 egg to the same pan and fry, breaking the yolk and gently forming the egg into a 7.5 x 7.5cm (3 x 3in) square. Repeat with the other egg and set aside.

Place a sheet of seaweed on a clean surface, shiny side down and longer side at the bottom. Fold in half, then in half again to quarter it (you should have a square). Unfold the seaweed and, using scissors, cut through one of the shorter folds between two squares, stopping at the centre point, then position that fold at the bottom. Wet your fingertips with water and spread half the rice evenly over the bottom right square, all the way to the edges.

Place half the Spam on the top left quadrant of seaweed. Place the egg on the top right. If using kkaennip, place one on the bottom right quadrant and top with half the kimchi. Fold each quadrant up in a clockwise direction, starting with the bottom left, to make a square wrap 'sandwich'. Repeat with the remaining ingredients.

Tuna, Cheese & Cucumber

Prep time: 25 minutes
Total time: 25 minutes

For the Rice

200g (1 cup) steamed short-grain
  white rice
1 tbsp roasted sesame oil
1 tsp roasted sesame seeds
sea or kosher salt

For the Filling

60g (¼ cup) drained tinned tuna
1 tbsp Kewpie mayonnaise
1 tsp roasted sesame oil
1 tsp roasted sesame seeds
¼ tsp fish sauce
2 cheese slices of your choice
4 leaves Lollo Rosso lettuce,
  trimmed, cleaned and dried
¼ cucumber, thinly sliced

To Assemble

2 gim (roasted seaweed) sheets,
  about 19 x 22cm (7½ x 8½in)

I absolutely love a good tuna fish salad, so I had to include this version.

Mix the rice with the sesame oil, sesame seeds and salt in a bowl. Set aside.

Mix together the tuna, mayonnaise, sesame oil, sesame seeds and fish sauce and set aside.

Place a sheet of seaweed on a clean surface, shiny side down and longer side at the bottom. Fold in half, then in half again to quarter it (you should have a square). Unfold the seaweed and, using scissors, cut through one of the shorter folds between two squares, stopping at the centre point, then position that fold at the bottom. Wet your fingertips with water and spread half the rice evenly over the bottom right square, all the way to the edges.

Place a slice of cheese on the top right quadrant of seaweed, then place the lettuce on the top left and half the tuna mixture on top of the lettuce. Place a few slices of cucumber on the remaining quadrant. Fold each quadrant up in a clockwise direction, starting with the bottom left, to make a square wrap 'sandwich'. Repeat with the remaining ingredients.

Beef Bulgogi, Kimchi, Danmuji & Lettuce

Prep time: 28 minutes
Total time: 30 minutes

For the Rice

200g (1 cup) steamed short-grain
    white rice
1 tbsp roasted sesame oil
1 tsp roasted sesame seeds
sea or kosher salt

For the Filling

15g (½oz) butter (optional)
75g (¼ cup) ripe cabbage kimchi (see
    page 56), chopped
¼ tsp caster (superfine) sugar
    (optional)
80g (2¾oz) The Best Bulgogi Beef
    (see page 86)
4 Lollo Rosso or butter lettuce leaves,
    trimmed, cleaned and dried
8 thin slices of danmuji (yellow
    pickled radish)

To Assemble

2 gim (roasted seaweed) sheets,
    about 19 x 22cm (7½ x 8½in)

Sautéing kimchi with a pinch of sugar and butter is optional. The butter and sugar just rounds out the kimchi flavour a bit, especially if it is very ripe.

Mix the rice with the sesame oil, sesame seeds and salt in a bowl. Set aside.

If sautéing the kimchi, heat a non-stick frying pan over a medium-high heat. Add the butter and melt until foaming, then add the kimchi and sugar and sauté for 2 minutes until the kimchi has wilted and slightly browned on the edges. Remove from heat and set aside.

Place a sheet of seaweed on a clean surface, shiny side down and longer side at the bottom. Fold in half, then in half again to quarter it (you should have a square). Unfold the seaweed and, using scissors, cut through one of the shorter folds between two squares, stopping at the centre point, then position that fold at the bottom. Wet your fingertips with water and spread half the rice evenly over the bottom right square, all the way to the edges.

Place a lettuce leaf on the upper two squares of seaweed and top one with half the bulgogi and the other with half the kimchi. Place half the danmuji on the remaining quadrant. Fold each quadrant up in a clockwise direction, starting with the bottom left, to make a square wrap 'sandwich'. Repeat with the remaining ingredients.

닭죽

SERVES 4

Prep time: 10 minutes
Total time: 30 minutes

bones from 1 leftover roast or
 rotisserie chicken
420g (3 cups) steamed short-grain
 white rice
1l (4 cups) chicken stock

<u>For the Toppings</u> (optional)

170g (6oz) roast or unflavoured
 rotisserie chicken meat, shredded
4 tbsp fried shallots
4 tsp chopped chives, sliced into 1cm
 (½in) lengths
¼ tsp black sesame seeds
3–4 tbsp cabbage kimchi (see page
 56), chopped
kkaesogeum (sesame seed salt)
gochugaru (Korean chilli flakes)
roasted sesame oil
soy sauce
sea or kosher salt

Magical Chicken Rice Porridge

Dak Juk

Whenever I was sick or even just sad, my mom would feed me juk, rice porridge. There is something so incredibly comforting and healing about this dish. It is warming to the soul, and wonderfully satisfying to eat too... and it always makes me feel better.

In a large heavy-based saucepan over a high heat, combine the chicken bones, rice and chicken stock, then bring to the boil while stirring occasionally. Lower the heat to medium-low and simmer for about 20 minutes, stirring the rice every 5 minutes to ensure it doesn't stick to the bottom. Simmer until the liquid is reduced and the rice is plump and broken.

Divide the rice porridge between bowls and garnish with shredded chicken and any other toppings of your choice. Serve immediately with soy sauce on the side or drizzled over.

<u>Tip</u>
You can also use microwaveable
precooked rice to save time.

호박죽

SERVES 4

Prep time: 10 minutes
Total time: 20 minutes

425g (15oz) tin of pumpkin purée
590ml (2½ cups) vegetable stock or
   water, plus extra for desired
   consistency
3 tbsp glutinous (sweet) rice flour,
   plus extra as needed
1–2 tbsp brown or white sugar, or
   to taste
1 tsp sea or kosher salt, or
   to taste

For the Rice Cake Balls

45g (¼ cup) glutinous (sweet) rice
   flour, plus extra as needed
⅛ tsp sea or kosher salt
2 tbsp hot water

To Serve

1 tbsp toasted pine nuts
4 tbsp tinned prepared red beans
   (whole beans, not purée)

Pumpkin Porridge

Hobak Juk

This silky, velvety porridge will hug you and make you feel warm and cozy from the inside out. Instead of roasting raw pumpkin, you can simply buy plain pumpkin or butternut squash purée as a starting point. Although the chewy rice cake balls are not essential, they do make a welcome lip-smacking addition to this pleasurable soup.

First, make the rice cake balls. In a medium bowl, mix together the rice flour and salt, then add the water, little by little; you may not need all of it. Once the mixture starts coming together into a dough, tip it out onto a clean surface dusted with rice flour. Knead lightly until it comes together uniformly and is springy to the touch. Add more flour as necessary to prevent sticking. Roll the dough out into a long rope, about 38cm (15in) long and about 1.5cm (¾in) thick, and cut using a knife into 1.5cm (¾in) pieces. Roll each piece into a small ball using the palms of your hands. You should have about 32 balls. If not cooking them right away, cover with cling film (plastic wrap) to prevent them drying out.

Place a small saucepan of water over a high heat. Bring to the boil, and drop in the rice balls. Cook for about 2 minutes until they float. Remove using a slotted spoon, place in a bowl with enough cold water to cover them and set aside.

Scoop the pumpkin purée into a medium saucepan over a medium-low heat. Whisk the stock or water with the rice flour in a small bowl, mixing together well. Add the rice mixture to the pumpkin and whisk until smooth. The texture should be thick and velvety. Add more water or a bit more rice flour if necessary. Mix in the sugar and salt to taste. You can use white sugar, if you like, as it will keep the juk bright orange. I like to use brown sugar as it adds a richer molasses taste and not just sweetness, although it does make the porridge a bit darker in colour. Once warmed through, turn off the heat, pour into serving bowls and add the rice balls. Garnish with toasted pine nuts and 1 tbsp of red beans per bowl. Serve immediately.

김치 볶음밥

SERVES 4

Prep time: 15 minutes
Total time: 30 minutes
  (varies based on protein used)

3 tbsp soy sauce
1½ tbsp Ssamjang (see page 194)
1 tbsp gochugaru (Korean chilli
  flakes)
1 tbsp caster (superfine) sugar
2 tbsp roasted sesame oil
vegetable or other neutral oil, for
  frying
2 spring onions (scallions), green and
  white parts, trimmed and thinly
  sliced
1 brown (yellow) onion, finely
  chopped
125g (1¼ cups) cabbage kimchi (see
  page 56) with juices, chopped into
  2cm (¾in) pieces (substitute with
  vegan kimchi if required)
1kg (5 cups) steamed short-grain
  white rice, dried out on a tray
60g (¼ cup) Kewpie mayonnaise
  (substitute with vegan mayonnaise
  if required)
sea or kosher salt
freshly ground black pepper

<u>To Serve</u> (optional)

1 spring onion (scallion), thinly sliced
  on a bias
gochugaru (Korean chilli flakes)

Kimchi Fried Rice

Kimchi-bokkeum-bap

Fried rice is traditionally made with leftover rice, but feel free to use freshly cooked rice dried out in the fridge overnight. I know there is controversy over how safe it is to heat up rice…but, us Asians have been doing it for centuries and we are okay! One of my chefs who worked with me at Jinjuu and Seoul Bird, Dana Choi, insists that classic kimchi fried rice only has kimchi and onions in it. This is her recipe below. The mayonnaise addition coats the rice grains, adding a nice creaminess.

Whisk together the soy sauce, ssamjang, gochugaru, sugar and sesame oil in a small bowl until well incorporated and the sugar is dissolved. Set aside.

Drizzle a little vegetable oil in a large non-stick frying pan over a medium-high heat. Add the spring onions and onion and sauté until softened and cooked through but not browned. Add the kimchi and stir-fry for about 2 minutes until softened. Add the rice and break it up, mixing it well with the kimchi and onions. Add the soy sauce mixture and mayonnaise and mix well to coat the rice, then cook for 3–4 minutes. Season with salt and pepper to taste then cook your protein (see page 134).

Remove from the heat, add the protein of your choice and mix well to incorporate. Spoon into bowls and top with the spring onions and a sprinkling of gochugaru, and serve immediately.

Kimchi Fried Rice Variations

Prawn (shrimp)

2 tbsp vegetable or other neutral oil
1 tsp grated garlic
12 medium raw prawns (shrimp),
   peeled, tail-on and deveined
sea or kosher salt
freshly ground black pepper

Place a medium non-stick frying pan over a medium heat and drizzle in the oil. Add the garlic and prawns and sauté for about 5 minutes until just cooked through. Remove from the pan and place into a bowl. Season with salt and pepper to taste, toss lightly and set aside.

Chicken

225g (8oz) boneless skinless chicken
   thighs, chopped into 1cm (½in)
   pieces
2 tbsp soy sauce
1 tsp roasted sesame oil
1 tsp grated garlic
2 tbsp vegetable or other neutral oil
sea or kosher salt
freshly ground black pepper

Toss the chicken in a bowl with the soy sauce, sesame oil and garlic. Mix to coat the chicken. Place a medium non-stick frying pan over a medium heat and drizzle in the vegetable oil. Add the chicken and all the marinade and sauté for about 8 minutes until cooked through. Remove the chicken from the pan and place into a bowl. Season with salt and pepper to taste, toss lightly and set aside.

Tofu

2 tbsp vegetable or other neutral oil
½ block extra-firm tofu (about
   225g/8oz), cut into 1cm (½in) dice
sea or kosher salt
freshly ground black pepper

Place a medium non-stick frying pan over a medium heat and drizzle in the oil. Gently dry the tofu well with a paper towel and add to the pan once the oil is hot. Sauté the tofu until golden brown, about 5 minutes. Season with salt and pepper and set aside.

비빔밥

───────

SERVES 4

Prep time: 20 minutes
Total time: 30 minutes
  (varies based on protein used)

For the 'Triple B' Sauce

110g (scant ½ cup) gochujang
  (Korean chilli paste)
2 tbsp mirim
1⅓ tbsp roasted sesame seeds
1⅓ tbsp roasted sesame oil
3 tbsp finely chopped spring onions
  (scallions)

For the Bibimbap

1 tbsp roasted sesame oil
800g (4 cups) steamed short-grain
  white rice
vegetable or other neutral oil, for
  cooking
100g (3½oz) soya bean sprouts (tails
  and any brown pieces removed) or
  mung bean sprouts
½ courgette (zucchini), halved
  lengthwise, then very sliced on a
  mandoline
1 carrot, peeled and julienned
180g (6½oz) spinach
4 shiitake mushrooms, destemmed
  and cut into 5mm (¼in) slices
115g (4oz) cabbage kimchi (see
  page 56), drained and cut into
  2cm (1in) pieces
1 large egg
sea or kosher salt

To Serve

roasted sesame seeds

Bountiful Bibimbap

Bibimbap

Bibimbap is one of the most iconic Korean dishes. A pinwheel of vegetables nuzzled in a bed of steamed rice, topped with your protein of choice – it is a whole balanced meal in a bowl.

You can use any leftover vegetables or banchan in your fridge, fresh lettuce or cucumber slices for crunch as well as beans or legumes, or add pre-sliced mushrooms and shredded carrots (use your food processor to speed up the process). Go seasonal when you can. There are no rules on what can go into bibimbap, which translates to 'mixed rice'. So have fun!

First make the 'Triple B' sauce. In a small bowl, stir together all the ingredients, until well incorporated, then set aside.

Next make the bibimbap. Place a heavy-based frying pan (preferably a cast-iron frying pan) over a medium heat. Add the sesame oil and gently spread the rice over the base of the frying pan in a loose layer. Cook, undisturbed, for 8–10 minutes until the bottom of the rice develops a golden crust.

Meanwhile, combine your protein with the marinade from the recipes on pages 136–38.

In a medium non-stick frying pan, heat 1 tsp of vegetable oil over a medium-high heat. Add the bean sprouts and cook, stirring, until crisp-tender, about 2 minutes. Season with salt to taste. Arrange the sprouts on the rice in a segment, resembling a triangular slice of pie or cheese. Repeat with all the vegetables, cooking each one separately: courgette (2 minutes), carrot (1 minute), spinach (2 minutes), then the mushrooms (2 minutes). It is best to do the mushrooms last to avoid discolouring the other ingredients with their dark juices. Arrange the kimchi on a section of the rice.

Cook your preferred protein (see pages 136–38).

Finally, add 1 tbsp of oil to the pan and fry the egg. Place the fried egg in the centre of the dish. Spoon the sauce next to the egg, or serve on the side in a small bowl. Sprinkle the bibimbap with sesame seeds. Bring the pan to the table, set it on a trivet and mix everything together before spooning into bowls.

Korean Mixed Rice Variations

Beef

3 tbsp soy sauce
1 tbsp roasted sesame oil
3 tbsp mirim
2 garlic cloves, grated
1 tsp grated ginger
1 tsp roasted sesame seeds, crushed
2 tsp caster (superfine) sugar
200g (7oz) bulgogi beef (Korean-style very thinly sliced meat) or ribeye, partially frozen and very thinly sliced
vegetable oil or other neutral oil, for cooking
sea or kosher salt
freshly ground black pepper

In a small bowl, stir together the soy sauce, sesame oil, mirim, garlic, ginger, sesame seeds and sugar. Whisk until the sugar is completely dissolved. Add the beef and mix well using your hands, massaging the marinade into the beef. Set aside.

Heat a drizzle of oil in a frying pan over a medium-high heat, add the meat (including all the sauce) and cook for 1–2 minutes until cooked through. Season with salt and pepper to taste. Arrange on the rice and spoon any juices from the pan over the meat.

Pork

2 tbsp gochujang (Korean chilli paste)
2 tsp doenjang (fermented soya bean paste)
2 tbsp mirim
2 tsp roasted sesame oil
1 tsp grated ginger
1 tsp grated garlic
140g (5oz) samgyeopsal (pork belly), thinly sliced or partially frozen skinless pork belly and thinly sliced
vegetable oil or other neutral oil, for cooking
sea or kosher salt
freshly ground black pepper

In a small bowl, whisk together the gochujang, doenjang, mirim, sesame oil, ginger and garlic. Add the pork and mix well using your hands to massage in the marinade well. Set aside.

Heat a drizzle of oil in a frying pan over a medium-high heat, add the meat (including all the sauce) and cook for 1–2 minutes until cooked through. Season with salt and pepper to taste. Arrange on the rice and spoon any juices from the pan over the meat.

Tofu

100g (3½oz) drained firm tofu, cut
  into 1cm (½in) cubes
sea or kosher salt
freshly ground black pepper

Place the tofu in a heatproof bowl and cover with a heatproof plate. Steam in the microwave on high for about 2 minutes until warmed through. Or place in a steamer and steam until warmed through, about 4 minutes.

One cooked through, drain and season with salt and pepper to taste.

Prawn (shrimp)

4 large garlic cloves, grated
1 tbsp soy sauce
1 tbsp vegetable oil
1 tbsp light brown sugar
sea or kosher salt
freshly ground black pepper
170g (6oz) raw prawns (shrimp),
  peeled and deveined

In a small bowl, mix together the garlic, soy sauce, oil, and sugar. Add the prawns and toss to coat. Place in the fridge until ready to cook.

Place a non-stick frying pan over a high heat. Add the prawns along with all the marinade and sauté until the sauce is sticky and the prawns are coated. Season with salt and pepper to taste. Arrange on the rice and spoon any juices from the pan over the prawns.

잡채

SERVES 6

Prep time: 15 minutes
Total time: 30 minutes
(varies based on protein used)

For the Seasoning Sauce

2 tbsp caster (superfine) sugar
4 tbsp roasted sesame oil
2 tbsp roasted sesame seeds,
   crushed
4 tbsp soy sauce
2 tsp sea or kosher salt
1½ tsp freshly ground black pepper

For the Noodles

300g (10½oz) dangmyeon (sweet
   potato noodles)
vegetable or other neutral oil,
   for frying
1 large brown (yellow) onion, thinly
   sliced
300g (10½oz) chestnut (cremini),
   button or shiitake mushrooms,
   destemmed and sliced
2 large carrots, julienned
285g (10oz) baby spinach
5 spring onions (scallions), cut into
   5cm (2in) pieces

For the Omelette Strips

2 large eggs, lightly beaten with a
   splash of water
pinch of sea or kosher salt

To Serve

3 tbsp shredded gim (roasted
   seaweed)
15g (½oz) enoki mushrooms
   (optional)

Unni's Favourite Stir-fried Sweet Potato Noodles

Japchae

My mom still makes japchae for every special occasion, and it is also my sister (unni in Korean) Sonya's favourite. It is the type of dish that you can make with all leftover vegetables or dress it up for a celebration. No matter what, it is always a crowd-pleaser. These springy, toothsome noodles are so gratifying. You can eat this dish warm or at room temperature. The most popular version is beef, but Sonya likes it with prawns (shrimp) the best, as it's the way our mom usually makes it!

For the seasoning sauce, mix together all the ingredients in a small bowl, whisking well until the sugar is dissolved. Set aside.

Bring a large saucepan of water to the boil. Add the dangmyeon noodles and cook according to the packet instructions until cooked through. Drain, rinse under cold water, then drain well in a colander, shaking to remove excess water. Cut through the noodles with kitchen scissors several times to prevent large tangles. Transfer to a large bowl or pan, tip in the seasoning sauce and toss until well coated. Set aside, mixing occasionally.

Make the omelette strips. In a medium bowl, beat the eggs with the salt. Place a medium non-stick frying pan over a medium-low heat and drizzle with oil. Pour the eggs into the pan, swirling to evenly coat the bottom. Cook slowly without disturbing until the egg is set but not browned on the bottom, about 2–3 minutes. You do not want to get any browning or colour on the egg. Once the egg is set on the bottom, flip and cook until done. Slide onto a cutting board. Carefully roll the egg into a log and cut crosswise into thin strips about 5mm (¼in) thick. Set aside.

Place a non-stick frying pan over a medium heat and drizzle with oil. Add the onion and cook, stirring often, until slightly softened, about 2 minutes. Add the mushrooms and carrots and cook until slightly softened then add the spinach and cook until wilted, about 2–3 minutes. Finally add the spring onions and cook until just wilted, about 1–2 minutes, then toss through the other vegetables. Transfer the vegetables to the bowl with the dangmyeon noodles. Mix well together.

Add your chosen variation (see page 140) then transfer the dangmyeon noodles to a plate and scatter the omelette strips on top. Garnish with the shredded gim and enoki mushrooms, then serve.

Stir-fried Sweet Potato Noodle Variations

Prawn (shrimp)

vegetable or other neutral oil, for frying

4 large garlic cloves, grated

700g (1lb 9oz) jumbo king prawns (shrimp), peeled (including tails, if desired), deveined and patted dry

1 tbsp fish sauce

1 tbsp mirim

sea or kosher salt

freshly ground black pepper

Place a non-stick frying pan over a medium-high heat and drizzle with oil. Add the garlic and cook, stirring often, until fragrant and just softened, about 10 seconds. Add the prawns and cook until barely pink, about 1–2 minutes. Add the fish sauce and mirim and cook, stirring often, until the prawns are cooked through, about 3 minutes more. Tip the prawns and juices into the noodles, season with salt and pepper to taste and mix well.

Chicken

vegetable or other neutral oil, for frying

4 large garlic cloves, grated

450g (1lb) boneless skinless chicken thighs, cut into thin strips (1 x 5cm/½ x 2in)

1 tbsp mirim

2 tbsp soy sauce

sea or kosher salt

freshly ground black pepper

Place a non-stick frying pan over a medium-high heat and drizzle with oil. Add the garlic and cook, stirring often, until fragrant and just softened, about 10 seconds. Add the chicken, mirim and soy sauce and cook, stirring often, until the chicken is cooked through, about 4–5 minutes. Tip the chicken and the juices into the noodles, season with salt and pepper to taste and mix well.

Beef

vegetable or other neutral oil, for frying

4 large garlic cloves, grated

1 tsp grated ginger

700g (1lb 9oz) bulgogi beef (Korean-style very thinly sliced meat) or ribeye, partially frozen and very thinly sliced

3 tbsp soy sauce

2 tbsp roasted sesame oil

3 tsp caster (superfine) sugar

sea or kosher salt

freshly ground black pepper

Place a non-stick frying pan over a medium-high heat and drizzle with oil. Add the garlic and ginger and cook, stirring often, until fragrant and just softened, about 10 seconds. Add the beef, soy sauce, sesame oil and sugar and cook, stirring often, until the beef is cooked through, about 6–7 minutes. Tip the beef and the juices into the noodles, season with salt and pepper to taste and mix well.

바지락 칼국수

Umma's Clam Knife-cut Noodles

Bajirak Kal-guksu

SERVES 2

Active time: 30 minutes
Total time: 1–2 hours, for clam
  soaking

300g (10½oz) fresh kal-guksu
  noodles
950ml (4 cups) Anchovy Dashi Stock
  (see page 192) or 1 tbsp anchovy
  dashida (Korean anchovy stock
  powder) dissolved in 950ml
  (4 cups) water
1 tbsp fish sauce
1 tsp grated garlic
½ courgette (zucchini), preferably a
  Korean courgette or aehobak
  julienned
½ brown (yellow) onion, thinly sliced
½ large carrot, peeled and julienned
12 littleneck clams, cleaned (shells
  scrubbed and clams soaked in cold,
  salted water for at least 1 hour and
  up to 3 hours to remove any sand)
2 spring onions (scallions), thinly
  sliced on a bias
sea or kosher salt
freshly ground black pepper

To Serve

sliced red chillis, preferably Korean
  but Fresnos will also work
Dadaegi Spicy Sauce (see page 190)

Kal-guksu translates to 'knife-cut noodle soup' and this homely bowl is oh so gratifying. My mom used to make a chicken version too, with a healing chicken broth and, of course, her homemade noodles. Nowadays, you can just buy these gratifying noodles fresh in the fridge section of Asian supermarkets. Feel free to use frozen or jarred clams as well.

Cook the noodles according to the packet instructions, then drain and set aside.

Meanwhile, place a large saucepan over a high heat and add the stock. Add the fish sauce and garlic. Once boiling, add the courgette, onion and carrot. Cook until the vegetables are just soft, about 3–4 minutes.

Add the clams and cook for about 4 minutes, until opened. Add the cooked noodles and stir well. Remove from the heat and add the spring onions. Season with salt and pepper to taste.

Garnish with red chillis. Serve immediately with the dadaegi spicy sauce on the side.

Tip

Buy packaged grated (shredded)
carrots to save time.

냉면

Appa's Ice-cold Noodles

Naengmyeon

SERVES 2

Prep time: 25 minutes
Total time: 30 minutes

2 portions of packaged naengmyeon,
  including broth sachets
ice cubes

For the Dressing

2 tbsp rice vinegar
1 tsp caster (superfine) sugar
1 tsp gyeoja (Korean hot mustard)
1 tsp gochugaru (Korean chilli flakes)
2 tsp roasted sesame seeds
sea or kosher salt
freshly ground black pepper

For the Salad

1 large Asian pear
½ cucumber
3 'sexy' spring onions (scallions)
  (follow step 1 on page 50)
30g (1oz) thinly sliced shallots
¼ red onion, thinly sliced

To Serve

1 quail egg, hard-boiled and halved
4 thin slices of roast beef, or leftover
  pot roast, cut into 5cm (2in) strips

My dad was born in Chŏngju, a small town in what is now North Korea, and he loves this cold dish, which also hails from North Korea. It contains long, thin noodles that are usually made from buckwheat, which are sold dried or fresh and often with a broth sachet tucked inside – a good brand is Pulmuone. Feel free to make this packaged broth ahead of time and partially freeze it until slushy; this avoids having to add ice cubes, which can dilute the soup.

Make the naengmyeon and the broth according to the packet instructions. Divide between two large bowls and top with ice cubes.

In a medium bowl, whisk the dressing ingredients together and set aside.

Use a mini melon baller or spoon to make balls out of the pear and the cucumber, then set aside. Add the pear and cucumber balls, spring onions, shallot rings and red onion to the bowl with the dressing and gently toss.

To serve, top the noodles with the roast beef, then the salad. Finish with a quail egg half.

짜장면

SERVES 4

Prep time: 5 minutes
Total time: 30 minutes

For the Noodles

2 tbsp potato starch
3 tbsp vegetable or other neutral oil
280g (10oz) skinless pork belly or
  beef ribeye, cut into 5mm (¼in)
  cubes
225g (8oz) brown (yellow) onions,
  diced
3 garlic cloves, grated
350g (12oz) potatoes, peeled and
  diced
125g (4½oz) courgette (zucchini)
  (preferably a Korean courgette or
  aehobak), diced
150g (5½oz) chunjang (black bean
  paste)
450g (1lb) fresh jjajangmyeon
  (Chinese-style wheat noodles)
1 tsp sea or kosher salt
freshly ground black pepper

For the Skewers

12 thin slices of danmuji (yellow
  pickled radish)
½ Persian (Kirby) cucumber, thinly
  sliced
1 small brown (yellow) onion,
  quartered

To Serve

½ courgette (zucchini), julienned
½ carrot, julienned
4 tbsp chunjang (black bean paste)
  mixed with 1 tbsp water
white vinegar

Noodles with Black Bean Sauce

Jjajangmyeon

My dad loves this Chinese-Korean dish – a cavernous bowl of noodles swimming in a black bean sauce, studded with bits of potato, courgettes (zucchini) and juicy cubes of pork. In Korea, this dish with a side of tangsuyuk (sweet and sour deep-fried beef) is by far the best delivery food option, period. It always comes piping hot in real serving bowls on trays. When you're done you simply leave the tray and bowls outside your door and the delivery person comes back to retrieve them later. If you don't use a fatty meat like pork belly or ribeye, add another tablespoon of oil when cooking the chunjang (black bean paste).

In a small glass, whisk the potato starch with 60ml (¼ cup) water and set aside.

Place a large non-stick frying pan over a medium–high heat. Drizzle in the oil and add the pork or beef, then cook for 6–7 minutes until browned on all sides and some fat has rendered.

Tip in the onions and garlic and cook for 3–4 minutes, stirring occasionally, until the onions have softened. Add the potatoes and courgette and cook for 3–4 minutes, stirring occasionally, until the potatoes start to soften. Stir in the black bean paste, salt and pepper to taste. Add 590ml (2½ cups) water and mix well. Simmer gently for 4–5 minutes. Stir in the potato starch mixture. Simmer for a further 10–12 minutes, stirring frequently, until the vegetables are cooked through and the sauce has thickened.

Meanwhile, cook the jjajangmyeon noodles according to the packet instructions (around 5–7 minutes), drain, rinse well and drain again. To serve, divide the sauce among four large bowls, then do the same with the noodles, making neat mounds on top of the sauce. Garnish with the carrot and courgette.

To make the skewers, fold the danmuji and cucumbers and pierce them onto skewers, alternating with the onion slices.

Serve the noodles with the danmuji, onion and cucumber skewers on the side. Pour the diluted chunjang in a small bowl for dipping and place alongside the skewers for dipping. Tip the vinegar into a small pouring jug and serve on the side too, as it is customary to pour a bit of vinegar on the noodles and mix well before eating.

쫄면

SERVES 2

Prep time: 24 minutes
Total time: 30 minutes

340g (12oz) soya bean sprouts (tails
  and any brown pieces removed)
400g (14oz) fresh or frozen jjolmyeon
  (Korean chewy wheat noodles)
½ cucumber, julienned
70g (2½oz) packaged coleslaw mix or
  3 large green cabbage leaves,
  shredded, and 30g (1oz) carrot,
  peeled and julienned

For the Sauce

3 tbsp gochugaru (Korean chilli
  flakes)
95g (⅓ cup) gochujang (Korean chilli
  paste)
2 tbsp caster (superfine) sugar
2 tbsp maesil cheong (plum extract)
3 tbsp rice vinegar
3 tbsp soy sauce
60g (¼ cup) apple purée
1 tbsp grated garlic
1 tbsp roasted sesame oil
1 tbsp roasted sesame seeds,
  crushed

To Serve

2 quail eggs, boiled to desired
  doneness and halved (optional)
kkaesogeum (sesame seed salt)
gochugaru (Korean chilli flakes)

Spicy, Chewy Cold Noodles

Jjolmyeon

Jjolmyeon means 'chewy noodles', and they are made from wheat flour and starch. This cold dish is so satiating – chewy noodles slathered in a sweet and spicy sauce. It is one of my mom's favourite bowls. If she does not have jjolmyeon noodles, she will just make this with spaghetti – it works great too.

Bring a large saucepan of water to the boil. Meanwhile, mix together all the ingredients for the sauce in a bowl and stir until well combined, then set aside.

Once the water is boiling, place the soya bean sprouts in the water and cook for 1 minute, then remove with a slotted spoon, rinse under cold water and set aside.

Bring the water back to the boil and cook the jjolmyeon noodles according to the packet instructions, making sure to stir often to separate them. Strain the noodles into a colander and rinse under cold running water while gently rubbing until cold, about 1 minute.

To serve, either mix the sauce with the jjolmyeon noodles or pour the sauce on top of the noodles, then top with the vegetables, boiled eggs (if using) a sprinkle of kkaesogeum and more gochugaru.

SOUPS

&

———STEWS

된장찌개

Doenjang Stew

Doenjang-jjigae

SERVES 2–4

Prep time: 15 minutes
Total time: 30 minutes

115g (4oz) frozen or fresh clams or
   clam meat
710ml (3 cups) Anchovy Dashi Stock
   (see page 192) or 1 tbsp anchovy
   dashida (Korean anchovy stock
   powder) dissolved in 710ml
   (3 cups) water
5–6 tbsp doenjang (fermented soya
   bean paste)
½ courgette (zucchini), cut into
   1–1.5cm (½–¾in) dice
1 small brown (yellow) onion, cut into
   1–1.5cm (½–¾in) dice
1 small Maris Piper (Yukon Gold)
   potato, peeled and cut into 1–1.5cm
   (½–¾in) dice
4 garlic cloves, grated
400–450g (14–16oz) block of firm
   tofu, drained and cut into 2.5cm
   (1in) cubes
2 spring onions (scallions), thinly
   sliced on a bias
1 green chilli, preferably Korean but a
   jalapeño will also work, deseeded
   and thinly sliced on a bias
1 red chilli, preferably Korean but a
   Fresno will also work, thinly sliced
   on a bias

To Serve

roasted sesame oil
3 'sexy' spring onions (scallions)
   (follow step 1 on page 50)
1 green chilli, deseeded and thinly
   sliced on a bias
1 red chilli, thinly sliced on a bias
steamed short-grain white rice

This umami-filled tasty stew is usually served alongside Korean barbecue.
I love the rich, complex flavours from the doenjang, clams and anchovy
stock. I have put in extra tofu, as it tastes so good after soaking up the
savoury stock. Definitely try to use a good-quality doenjang, as it is the
main flavour of this dish.

If using fresh clams, clean and place them in a bowl of cold salted water
to release any sand. Leave in the fridge and allow to soak for at least
15 minutes or overnight. Drain before using.

In a medium heavy-based saucepan, pour in the anchovy stock and bring to
the boil over a high heat. Add 5 tbsp of the doenjang and whisk until
dissolved. Taste the stock, and if you'd like a stronger doenjang flavour,
whisk in a little more. Add the courgette, onion, potato and garlic and
simmer for about 5 minutes more until the vegetables are just tender. Add
the clams or clam meat, cover and simmer 3–4 minutes until just cooked.
Note: if using fresh clams, the shells will open fully when done.

Add the tofu, spring onions and green and red chillis and simmer,
uncovered, until warmed through, about 2 minutes.

To serve, lightly drizzle with sesame oil and garnish with the spring onions
and a few more slices of green and red chilli. Accompany with steamed rice.

김치찌개

SERVES 4

Prep time: 7 minutes
Total time: 30 minutes

1 tbsp vegetable or other neutral oil
280g (10oz) skinless boneless pork
   belly, cut crosswise into 5cm (2in)
   pieces then lengthwise into 5mm
   (¼in) slices
450g (3 cups) drained very ripe
   cabbage kimchi (see page 56)
   or shop-bought kimchi, coarsely
   chopped
60ml (¼ cup) ripe kimchi juice
½ brown (yellow) onion, diced
830ml (3½ cups) Anchovy Dashi
   Stock (see page 192) or chicken
   stock, or 1 tbsp anchovy dashida
   (Korean anchovy stock powder)
   dissolved in 830ml (3½ cups) water
400g (14oz) firm tofu, drained, cut
   lengthwise into 1cm (½in) cubes
1 red chilli, preferably Korean but a
   Fresno will also work, deseeded and
   thinly sliced on a bias
pinch of sea or kosher salt

To Serve

1 red chilli, thinly sliced on a bias
4 chives, sliced into 2cm (1in) lengths
roasted sesame oil
steamed short-grain white rice

Warming Kimchi Stew

Kimchi-jiggae

My dear friend, Joyce, makes this soothing stew often during cold, snowy months. This funky pot tends to stink up your kitchen, but the resultant thick, tangy broth is so deeply comforting, it's worth any lingering stench. Use extra-ripe sour kimchi, as this soup should have vigour and gusto. If you cannot find anything suitable, sauté under-ripe kimchi with the pork until softened and add a splash of vinegar to make up the tanginess. Even though it's freezing outside, Joyce always opens her windows to air out her apartment after eating this stew... but, as the stew is so warming, she doesn't mind.

In a medium saucepan, heat the oil over a medium heat. Add the pork and cook for about 5 minutes until some of the fat has rendered and the meat is mostly no longer pink. Increase the heat to medium-high, add the kimchi, kimchi juice, onion and salt, and stir to combine. Add the stock and bring to the boil over a high heat, stirring often. Reduce the heat and simmer for 15 minutes.

After 15 minutes, add the tofu and cook to heat through for 2–3 minutes, then stir in the chilli. Taste and add more salt, if necessary. Transfer to a serving bowl, drizzle with sesame oil, scatter with chopped chives and red chillis then serve with steamed rice.

Army Base Stew

부대찌개

Budae-jjigae

SERVES 4

Prep time: 15 minutes
Total time: 30 minutes

12-16 pieces tteokgukyong-tteok (Korean oval sliced rice cakes)
vegetable or other neutral oil, for cooking
225g (8oz) skinless boneless pork belly slices, about 1cm (½in) thick, cut into 2.5cm (1in) wide pieces
225g (1½ cup) drained very ripe cabbage kimchi (see page 56) or shop-bought kimchi, coarsely chopped
1 tbsp gochugaru (Korean chilli flakes)
60ml (¼ cup) ripe kimchi juice
½ brown (yellow) onion, sliced
170g (6oz) Spam, cut into 2.5cm (1in) pieces (alternatively, you can use ham)
1 hot dog sausage, cut into 2.5cm (1in) pieces on a bias
1 tbsp gochujang (Korean chilli paste)
2 tsp soy sauce
2 tbsp grated garlic
1 packet of spicy instant ramen, including broth sachet
1.9l (8 cups) Anchovy Dashi Stock (see page 192) or 2 tbsp anchovy dashida (Korean anchovy stock powder) dissolved in 1.9l (8 cups) water
200g (7oz) tofu, cut into 2cm (1in) cubes
2 spring onions (scallions), thinly sliced
150g (5½oz) tin of baked beans (optional)
2–3 slices of American cheese

Budae-jjigae is a dish that was invented in the 1950s during the Korean War. During this time, Korea was one of the poorest countries in the world. This humble bowl, created out of scarcity, was concocted out of any available army rations, which were stewed in a spicy broth. Ingredients could include: Spam, Vienna sausages, American cheese slices, macaroni, instant ramen, luncheon meats, baked beans and more. I'm not going THAT hardcore authentic in my recipe below... but, I had to include the Spam!

Place the tteok in a bowl and add enough warm water just to cover. Set aside.

Place a large, wide saucepan over a medium-high heat. Drizzle in a little oil, then add the pork belly and kimchi and cook for about 5 minutes until the pork is cooked through. Add the gochugaru and sauté to coat the pork. Add the kimchi juice, onion, Spam, hot dog slices, drained rice cakes, gochujang, soy sauce, garlic, ramen broth sachet and pour the dashi stock on top. Let it come to the boil, then add the tofu, spring onions, ramen noodles and baked beans (if using) and boil for 2 minutes. Finally, add the American cheese and cook for another minute until the ramen is fully cooked. Serve immediately.

야채 순두부찌개

Vegetarian Silken Tofu Stew

Yachae Sundubu-jjigae

SERVES 4

Prep time: 10 minutes
Total time: 30 minutes

1 tbsp vegetable or other neutral oil
½ brown (yellow) onion, diced
150g (1 cup) ripe vegan cabbage
  kimchi (see page 56), diced
2 tbsp gochugaru (Korean chilli
  flakes)
2 garlic cloves, grated
2 tbsp Ssamjang (see page 194)
480ml (2 cups) vegetable dashi stock
  (see page 193)
1 small courgette (zucchini), halved
  lengthwise and cut into 1cm (½in)
  slices
100g (3½oz) sliced assorted
  mushrooms (any mixture of button,
  enoki, oyster, shiitake)
400g (14oz) silken tofu, drained
1 large egg (optional)
sea or kosher salt

To Serve

1 green chilli, preferably Korean but a
  jalapeño will also work
  thinly sliced

There are so many variations of this beloved silky spiced stew. I usually make an extra-spicy version with clams and kimchi. This version below is plant-forward, with vegan kimchi and ssamjang boosting the flavour profile greatly. If you're not vegetarian, feel free to add your protein of choice.

Heat the oil in a medium heavy-based saucepan over a medium-low heat. Add the onion, kimchi and gochugaru and cook, stirring occasionally, for about 5 minutes until the onion is just softened. Stir in the garlic and ssamjang, then add the stock and bring to a simmer over a medium-high heat. Add the courgette and mushrooms and bring to the boil. Reduce to a simmer and cook until the vegetables are softened, about 5 minutes.

Carefully add the tofu in chunks, season with salt to taste and gently stir, trying to keep the tofu intact as much as possible. When the tofu is heated through, crack an egg into the saucepan (if using) and gently mix it into the stew. Remove the stew from the heat, ladle into bowls and top with green chilli. Serve immediately.

떡국

SERVES 4

Prep time: 15 minutes
Total time: 30 minutes

450g (1lb) tteokgukyong-tteok
  (Korean oval sliced rice cakes)
1 tsp vegetable or other neutral oil
225g (8oz) minced (ground) beef
1.9l (8 cups) beef bone broth or
  3 tbsp beef dashida (Korean beef
  stock powder) dissolved in 1.9l
  (8 cups) water
2 large eggs, beaten with a splash of
  water
sea or kosher salt
freshly ground black pepper

To Serve

3 large eggs (optional)
large handful of spring onions
  (scallions), thinly sliced on a bias
kkaesogeum (sesame seed salt)
3 gim (roasted seaweed) sheets,
  shredded (optional)

My Cousin Eugene's Favourite Rice Cake Soup

Tteokguk

This nourishing soup is my cousin Eugene's favourite, although he prefers it with dumplings added in – do feel free to add the meat and mushroom dumplings from page 95 or any shop-bought ones. It is tradition to eat this gratifying bowl every New Year's Day, as it brings good luck. The sliced tteok represent coins, symbolising good fortune, and the white colour of the rice cakes signifies purity and a clean start to the new year ahead.

Place the tteok in a bowl and add enough warm water just to cover. Set aside.

Make the omelette strips to serve (if using). In a medium bowl, beat the three eggs with a splash of water and a pinch of salt. Place a medium non-stick frying pan over a medium-low heat and drizzle with oil. Pour the eggs into the pan, swirling to evenly coat the bottom. Cook slowly without disturbing until the egg is set but not browned on the bottom, about 2–3 minutes. You do not want to get any browning or colour on the egg. Once the egg is set on the bottom, flip and cook until done. Slide onto a cutting board. Carefully roll the egg into a log and cut crosswise into thin strips about 5mm (¼in) thick. Set aside.

Add the beef to the same pan. Break it up and cook it for 5–7 minutes until golden brown. While the beef is browning, bring the stock to the boil in a large saucepan over a high heat.

Once the stock is boiling, add the beef and drained rice cakes and simmer for about 2 minutes until the rice cakes are soft.

Drizzle the eggs into the broth while the soup is at a low simmer, stir gently and remove from the heat. Season the soup with salt and pepper to taste. Divide the soup between bowls and top with the omelette strips, spring onions, kkaesogeum and shredded gim (if using), then serve immediately.

콩나물국

SERVES 4

Prep time: 15 minutes
Total time: 20 minutes

280g (10oz) soya bean sprouts (tails and any brown pieces removed)
2 tbsp grated garlic
2 tbsp soy sauce
1 tbsp fish sauce
½ tsp gochugaru (Korean chilli flakes) (optional)
2 spring onions (scallions), thinly sliced
sea or kosher salt
freshly ground black pepper

To Serve
roasted sesame seeds

Soya Bean Sprout Soup

Kongnamulguk

I relish in the simplicity of this clean, clear soup, which allows the humble soya bean sprout to shine. My mom used to make huge pots of it. She didn't always have time to pick off the soya bean's wiry roots, so they would get tangled and form lumpy masses. I didn't mind though, as I liked to munch my way through these soya bean hordes... so scrumptious.

I love eating this nourishing soup for breakfast, with a heaping scoop of sticky white rice mixed in and a bowl of ripe kimchi on the side. You can use homemade dashi stock (see pages 192–93) instead of water if you like.

Bring about 2l (9 cups) of water to the boil in a large saucepan. Once boiling, add the soya bean sprouts along with the garlic, soy sauce and fish sauce. Let it boil until the bean sprouts are tender, about 5 minutes. Add salt to taste, along with the gochugaru (if using). Remove from the heat, add the spring onions, sprinkle with sesame seeds and serve.

육개장

SERVES 2–4

Prep time: 10 minutes
Total time: 30 minutes

115g (4oz) dangmyeon (sweet potato noodles)

2 tbsp vegetable or other neutral oil

2 tbsp roasted sesame oil

450g (1lb) bulgogi beef (Korean-style, very thinly sliced meat) or ribeye or sirloin, partially frozen and sliced into 2.5–5cm (1–2in) strips

6 spring onions (scallions), halved lengthwise, green and white parts separated, and cut into 5cm (2in) pieces

½ brown (yellow) onion, cut into 1cm (½in) slices

2 tsp sea or kosher salt, plus more to taste

25g (¼ cup) gochugaru (Korean chilli flakes)

100g (3½oz) shimeji or oyster mushrooms, torn into 1cm (½in) pieces

80g (2¾oz) shiitake mushrooms, destemmed and caps sliced into 1cm (½in) pieces

200g (1½ cups) packaged, pre-soaked, drained gosari namul (fern bracken), cut into 7cm (3in) pieces

80ml (⅓ cup) soy sauce

3 tbsp grated garlic

2 tbsp beef dashida (Korean beef stock powder)

210g (7½oz) mung bean sprouts

3 large eggs

freshly ground black pepper

To Serve

'sexy' spring onions (scallions)

45g (1½oz) shimeji mushrooms

steamed short-grain white rice

Jessica's Spicy Beef Soup

Yookgaejang

My recipe developer, Jessica Do, loves this hearty and meaty soup filled with spring onions (scallions). She made it all the time for her family during the pandemic to keep the plague away. If you cannot find gosari (fern bracken) namul, add more mushrooms and mung bean sprouts. Gosari namul bracken can be found in the fridge section of Asian supermarkets, sold in bags and packed with water. If you can only find dried gosari, you will need to rehydrate the ferns by boiling and soaking them in water, changing the liquid often.

In a large bowl, soak the dangmyeon noodles in warm water and set aside.

Place a large saucepan over a high heat and drizzle in the vegetable and sesame oil. Add the beef, spring onion whites, onion, and half the salt and sauté for 3–4 minutes until the beef is cooked through. Add the gochugaru and sauté everything while mixing for 1–2 minutes.

Add 1.9l (8 cups) water to the pan along with the mushrooms, drained gosari, soy sauce, garlic, the remaining salt and beef dashida. Cover with a lid and bring it to the boil for 8 minutes.

Drain and add the dangmyeon noodles to the pan along with the mung bean sprouts. Boil until the dangmyeon are cooked through, about 3–4 minutes. Then, add the spring onion greens. Crack the eggs into a separate bowl and whisk. While the stew is boiling, drizzle in the whisked eggs and stir gently, allowing the eggs to fully cook. Taste and add more salt and pepper to taste. Top with 'sexy' spring onions and a few fresh shimeji mushrooms. Serve with steamed white rice.

—DESSERTS

바노피 미숫가루 간장 카라멜 타르트

MAKES 1 X 22CM (9IN) PIE

Prep time: 30 minutes
Total time: 30 minutes

275ml (1 cup) dulce de leche
1 x 22cm (9in) pre-made digestive
  biscuit (graham cracker) pie crust or
  pre-baked sweet pie case of
  your choice
4 large ripe bananas, peeled and
  sliced about 5mm (¼in) thick
3 tbsp dark (75% cocoa solids)
  chocolate shavings
misutgaru, for dusting

For the Whipped Cream

480ml (2 cups) chilled double (heavy)
  cream
1 tsp vanilla extract
1 tsp instant coffee granules
1 tbsp icing (confectioners') sugar

For the Bruléed Bananas

2–3 bananas, sliced on a bias about
  1cm (½in) thick
70g (2½oz) granulated or caster
  (superfine) sugar

For the Soy Caramel

80g (¼ cup) shop-bought
  caramel sauce
2 tsp soy sauce

Banoffee Misutgaru & Soy Caramel Pie

Banopi Misutgaru Ganjang Karamel Tareuteu

Misutgaru is a nutty multigrain drink mix that I am obsessed with. Here, I've dusted it on top of this classic English dessert. The earthy and nutty notes of the misutgaru marry lovingly with the sweet dulce de leche and salty soy caramel. Fresh bananas delicately lift this pie to euphoric levels.

Tip the dulce de leche into a heatproof bowl and microwave on high for 1–2 minutes. Spoon the dulce de leche into the pie crust and spread into an even layer. Add the sliced bananas in a relatively even layer (they should overlap). Chill the pie while you make the whipped cream.

Using a hand mixer or stand mixer fitted with a whisk attachment, whip the double cream, vanilla extract, instant coffee and icing sugar on medium-high speed until firm peaks form, about 1–2 minutes, making sure not to over-whip.

Spread the whipped cream on top of the bananas, making sure to spread it to the edge and totally cover the bananas (this will help prevent them from browning). Chill the pie in the fridge again.

For the bruléed bananas, lay the sliced bananas on a non-stick baking sheet or tray in a single layer and sprinkle the sugar evenly on top until covered. Use a blowtorch to grill the bananas (or place in the oven under the grill (broiler) on high heat) until the sugar has caramelized and charred a bit.

Make the soy caramel by mixing the caramel and soy sauce until completely incorporated.

To serve, sprinkle the pie with chocolate shavings. Garnish with a dusting of misutgaru, the caramelized bananas slices and drizzle with the soy caramel. The pie can be kept chilled for up to 2 days.

달고나

MAKES 6 CANDIES

Prep time: 30 minutes
Total time: 30 minutes

6 tbsp caster (superfine) sugar
bicarbonate of soda (baking soda)

Korean Honeycomb Candy

Dalgona

The massively popular K-drama *Squid Games* ushered this old-fashioned street candy from Korea into the limelight. Traditionally, if you could successfully remove the pressed-in shape from the honeycomb disc without breaking it, the vendor would give you another one for free. It's a great dinner party activity! Use the honeycomb as a crunchy topping for ice cream!

The process for making these candies is quick and straightforward but it is important to make one candy at a time, as the method will not work if you melt all of the sugar at once.

Hold a copper dalgona ladle or stainless-steel ladle over a medium–low heat. Add 1 tbsp sugar and melt until it is just fully dissolved and still pale, stirring with a wooden chopstick.

Off the heat, add the smallest pinch of bicarbonate of soda and quickly stir with a wooden chopstick until the mixture lightens and foams a little. Immediately pour the mixture onto a non-stick baking sheet or a silicone baking mat. Flatten immediately with a press or flat metal spatula that has been sprayed or coated with oil. Remove the press, then quickly use a cookie cutter to gently mark a shape in the honeycomb, making sure not to press completely through. Remove the cutter and let the honeycomb cool for a further 20 seconds. Repeat five more times. Store the dalgona in an airtight container.

사과만두튀김

Fried Apple Dumplings

Sagwa Mandu Twigim

MAKES 16 DUMPLINGS

Prep time: 9 minutes
Total time: 30 minute

250g (1 cup) tinned apple-pie filling
25g (1oz) unsalted butter
1 Granny Smith apple, peeled, cored
  and chopped into 5mm (¼in) dice
1 tsp lemon juice
zest of 1 lemon
½ tsp vanilla extract, or to taste
pinch of sea or kosher salt
16 round dumpling wrappers
vegetable or other neutral oil, for
  deep-frying

For the Cinnamon Sugar

1 tbsp ground cinnamon
50g (¼ cup) caster (superfine) sugar

To Serve (optional)

vanilla ice cream
strawberry-flavoured Pepero sticks
pink mini marshmallows

Dumpling wrappers can be stuffed with absolutely anything. We used to serve a variation of this dessert in my old restaurant, Jinjuu – we even made a speciality cardboard sleeve reminiscent of the one used for the McDonald's fried apple pie. As shop-bought apple pie mix can taste vastly different, sample the filling and adjust to your liking, adding more lemon, cinnamon, vanilla, etc. When fried, bronzed and crispy, these delectable parcels never disappoint.

Blend the apple pie filling in a food processor until the apple pieces are small, similar to the chopped apple.

In a non-stick frying pan, melt the butter over a medium-high heat for about 1 minute until foaming. Add the chopped apples and cook while stirring until tender, about 2 minutes. Add the blended apple pie filling, lemon juice, zest and vanilla extract, mixing well to combine, then cook until sticky, about 2–3 minutes. Add the salt and mix well. Remove from the heat and set aside to cool. You can speed up the cooling process by putting the filling in a metal bowl over an ice bath, then stirring the mixture until the apples are cool to the touch.

Line a baking sheet with baking parchment then set up your dumpling-making station. Have a small bowl of water, filling and dumpling wrappers ready. Place about ¾–1 tbsp of filling in each dumpling wrapper, flour side up, then dip a finger in the cold water, dampen the edge of the dumpling wrapper and fold it over. You can add crimps, if you like. Place each folded dumpling on a baking sheet and cover with a slightly damp piece of paper towel or cling film (plastic wrap). Repeat until all the dumpling wrappers and all the filling is used up.

Meanwhile, heat a large saucepan of oil to 180°C (350°F). Fry the dumplings in batches of four or five for about 5 minutes until they are golden brown and crispy. Remove from the oil with a slotted spoon and place on a wire rack set over a baking sheet. Repeat with the rest of the dumplings.

Mix the cinnamon and sugar together in a small bowl. Toss the dumplings in the cinnamon sugar to coat.

Place a few scoops of ice cream in a bowl and top with the dumplings. Add a couple of Pepero sticks and a few mini marshmallows to serve, or whatever toppings you prefer.

Hotteok Crispy Rice Treats

Hotteok Raiseukeuriseupi

MAKES 12–16 TREATS

Prep time: 20 minutes
Total time: 30 minutes

non-stick spray or a little neutral oil,
  to coat the dish
85g (3oz) unsalted butter
4 tsp white miso paste
2 tsp ground cinnamon
1 tsp vanilla extract
285g (10oz) mini marshmallows
165g (5¾oz) crispy rice cereal
45g (1½oz) dry roasted peanuts,
  chopped

For the Chocolate Drizzle (optional)
85g (3oz) dark chocolate chips
1½ tsp coconut oil

These crispy rice treats are inspired by the flavours of classic hotteok, a traditional flat doughnut stuffed with cinnamon sugar and peanuts. In this recipe, I have added miso paste for an umami kick and used salted dry roasted peanuts to cut through the sweetness of the marshmallows. It may sound weird, but I assure you, you'll love this version of this iconic childhood snack.

Grease a 22 x 22cm (9 x 9in) baking dish (or smaller/larger size if you want thinner/thicker treats) with non-stick spray or a thin layer of oil and line generously with baking parchment so that it overhangs the edge of the dish. This makes it easy to take the crispy rice treats out of the dish.

In a large ovenproof non-stick frying pan, melt the butter with the miso paste over a medium heat, about 1 minute. Once melted, stir in the cinnamon and vanilla extract. Place the marshmallows in the pan and arrange in one layer. Toast the marshmallows using a blowtorch or place the frying pan under the grill (broiler) on high and toast until dark golden brown and slightly charred around the edges. This toasting will give the hotteok a roasted flavour. Place the pan back on the stove over a medium-low heat and stir, using a rubber spatula, until the marshmallows have completely melted, about 2 minutes.

Turn off the heat, add the cereal and peanuts and stir until well coated. Scrape the mixture into the greased baking dish and press firmly with a non-stick spatula to flatten it. Place another piece of baking parchment over the crispy rice cereal and press again to flatten evenly. Leave to cool for at least 10 minutes.

If making the chocolate drizzle, place the chocolate chips and coconut oil in a medium heatproof bowl and melt in the microwave on low power for 45–60 seconds, mixing occasionally, until smooth and fully melted. Set aside.

Once the treats are cool, use a knife to release the edges of the pan then remove them from the dish and place on a cutting board. Cut to your preferred size, drizzle with the melted chocolate (if using) and serve.

Strawberry Yakult Granita Shaved Ice

딸기 야쿠르트
고라니타방수

SERVES 2–4

Ttalgi Yakureuteu Geuranita Bingsu

Active time: 30 minutes
Total time: 4–8 hours, for freezing

8 x 65ml (2fl oz) Yakult bottles
300g (11oz) frozen strawberries,
   quartered

For the Toppings (optional)
150g (5½oz) strawberries, sliced
150g (5½oz) seedless green grapes,
   sliced
140g (1 cup) injeolmi (Korean rice
   cakes) or mini mochi, cut into 1cm
   (½in) pieces
gummy sweets (candy)
sweetened condensed milk

Growing up, our fridge was always stocked with rows of Yakult bottles. On hot summer days, my mom would sometimes place a few in the freezer. These tangy, yoghurt-like drinks freeze wonderfully, and their soft plastic bottles could be peeled off in a circular motion, like an orange rind, allowing me to enjoy the moulded ice like an ice pop. Inspired by this nostalgic treat, I've created a granita using this milky, sentimental sip, enhanced with the flavour of rosy strawberries.

Blend the Yakult, frozen strawberries and 200ml (½ cup) water in a blender until smooth. Pour the mixture into a 22 x 33cm (9 x 13in) metal or glass baking dish and place in the freezer. Freeze for at least 4 hours, or overnight.

When frozen, remove from the freezer and quickly scrape with a fork to create a granita texture. To serve, place the granita in a tall mound in a small bowl and top with the garnishes of your choice: strawberries, grapes, mochi and gummy sweets. Drizzle sweetened condensed milk on top. Serve immediately.

MAKES 12 TARTLETS

Active time: 30 minutes
Total time: 2 hours, for chilling

12 x 9cm (3½in) pre-made digestive
  biscuit (graham cracker) tarlet
  cases
340g (12oz) full-fat cream cheese
80g (⅔ cup) icing (confectioners')
  sugar
1 tbsp vanilla extract
500g (2 cups) full-fat Greek yoghurt
zest of ½ lemon
160ml (⅔ cup) double (heavy) cream,
  chilled
125ml (½ cup) yujacha (Korean citron
  tea syrup)

Yujacha No-bake Cheesecake Tartlets

Yujacha Chijeukeikeu Tareuteuret

Having spent my formative years in New York City, I harbour a strong hankering for cheesecake. Making a traditional NY-style cheesecake can be tricky, though, and requires a lot of patience and time (not to mention skill). Hence, I offer the effortless no-bake version below. Okay, I know it's not as deliciously dense as its NY counterpart, but it is pleasingly light and custardy. The oh-so-fragrant yujacha topping makes this tart a sure winner.

Place the tartlet cases on a baking sheet. Using a stand mixer fitted with the paddle attachment, beat the cream cheese, half the sugar and the vanilla extract until combined and fluffy. Add the yoghurt and lemon zest and beat for another minute. Set aside.

Fit the mixer with the whisk attachment and pour the cream and remaining sugar into a clean bowl. Whisk until stiff peaks form.

Gently fold the whipped cream into the cream cheese mixture. Spoon the filling into the tartlet cases. Place the tray in the fridge and chill until firm, about 2 hours.

Place the yujacha in a bowl and loosen with about 2 tbsp of hot water, mixing well. Just before serving, spoon a bit of the loosened yujacha over the tops of the tarts. Serve immediately.

수박화채

Watermelon Punch

Subak Hwaechae

SERVES 4

Prep time: 15 minutes
Total time: 15 minutes

1 mini watermelon, cut into 2.5cm (1in) chunks or shapes and seeds removed
150g (5½oz) seedless green grapes, halved
75g (2½oz) blackberries or blueberries, halved
2 cans of lemon-lime soda (e.g. Sprite, 7-Up or Chilsung Cider)
250ml (1 cup) whole milk
2 x 65ml (2fl oz) Yakult bottles
ice cubes

To Serve

Melona bar lollies (popsicles), or any other ice cream bar (optional)

When I was growing up, summertime meant watermelon season and my parents would inevitably lug home one of these gargantuan dark green melons. My dad would carve up the fruit with surgical skill, while my sister and I would happily inhale the crimson honeyed flesh. This invigorating punch blends lemon-lime soda, milk and yoghurty Yakult.

Hwaechae can also be made with any fruity or flowery tea, and you can add any tinned fruit or fruit cocktail mix. Feel free to also add condensed milk as well for added sweetness and creaminess. It is best that all the ingredients are ice-cold. If you like, cut the watermelon in half, scoop out the fruit, then use the empty shell as a punch bowl. Lop off a bit of the rounded bottom to make it flat so it stands easily. Hwaechae has gone viral on social media, and when you make it you will see why!

Place all the ingredients in a large punch bowl and stir. Serve with Melona bars and even use the ice cream bars as an alternative to ice. Serve immediately.

달고나커피

MAKES 1 TALL CUP

Prep time: 10 minutes
Total time: 10 minutes

2 tbsp instant coffee
2 tbsp caster (superfine) sugar
250ml (1 cup) whole milk (or your
    milk of choice), chilled
ice

Dalgona
Coffee

Dalgona Keopi

Korea is coffee crazy, and café culture is a real thing in Seoul. Cafés will stay open until late at night, and are seen, like bars, as places to hang out and socialize. This 'hand-beaten coffee', as it is also known, was invented in Macau. It eventually spread to Korea, where this consoling cuppa was rebranded as 'dalgona' when an actor quipped that it tasted just like the candy (see page 174). We've tested this several times and you get the best results when you use a common, no-brand instant coffee. No need to use anything fancy! You can also use a stand mixer to whip up this delicious frothy drink.

Place the instant coffee, sugar and 2 tbsp cold water in a small bowl then, using a hand mixer, whisk together for 5–7 minutes until extremely frothy. You can also do this in a blender or with a milk frother.

Pour the milk and ice into a tall glass and top with the whipped coffee. Stir before drinking and enjoy.

SAUCES &

—STOCKS

다대기

Dadaegi
Spicy Sauce

MAKES 60ML (¼ CUP)

Total time: 5 minutes

1 tbsp soy sauce
1 tsp gochugaru (Korean chilli flakes)
1 tsp thinly sliced green chillis,
   preferably Korean but jalapeños will
   also work
1 tsp rice vinegar
1 spring onion (scallion), thinly sliced
1 tsp roasted sesame oil
¼ tsp caster (superfine) sugar
½ tsp mirim
½ tsp roasted sesame seeds

I love this red fiery-hot sauce that is used mostly for noodles, stews and soups. Just stir in a generous spoonful to make any dish sing. I like it in knife-cut noodles (see page 143) or even instant ramen noodles. You can omit the fresh chillis, if you prefer a milder sauce.

Stir together all the ingredients in a small bowl and serve.

The sauce can be stored in an airtight container in the fridge for up to 2 weeks.

초장

Umma Do's Chojang

MAKES 80ML (⅓ CUP)

Total time: 5 minutes

2 tbsp gochujang (Korean chilli paste)
1½ tbsp rice vinegar
½ tbsp caster (superfine) sugar, or to
   taste
½ tbsp maesil cheong (plum extract)
   (optional)
1 tsp grated garlic
1 tsp roasted sesame seeds

Below is Jessica Do's mom's chojang recipe to accompany her famous Seafood Pancakes (see page 113). This spicy, sweet and vinegary sauce is mostly served with seafood dishes… but, goes well with almost anything. Try drizzling it over vegetables, on bibimbap, or as a dip for prawn cocktail or sashimi.

Stir together all the ingredients in a small bowl and serve.

The sauce can be stored in an airtight container in the fridge for up to 2 weeks.

기름장

Sesame Oil Dipping Salt

Total time: 2 minutes

4 tbsp roasted sesame oil
1 tsp sea, kosher salt or Korean solar salt
1 tsp freshly ground black pepper

This uber-simple dipping sauce is actually one of my favourites. I love the toasty nuttiness of roasted sesame oil. Serve this with any Korean barbecue. Do make sure you are using 100% pure, good-quality sesame oil, as this amber-coloured liquid gold is where all the flavour lies.

Divide the sesame oil between four small dipping dishes, then divide the salt and pepper between each one.

The dipping salt can be stored in an airtight container at room temperature for up to 2 weeks or in the fridge for up to 3 weeks.

고추장 마요네즈

MAKES 60ML (¼ CUP)

Gochujang Mayo

Total time: 5 minutes

60ml (¼ cup) Kewpie mayonnaise (or your favourite mayonnaise)
½ tsp caster (superfine) sugar, or to taste
½ tbsp gochujang (Korean chilli paste), or to taste

This spiced creamy mayo works well with literally anything. Slather on burgers, use as a dip for French fries, or put in a submarine sandwich. Do try to use Kewpie mayo, as it adds a welcome tanginess.

In a small bowl, mix together the mayonnaise, sugar and the gochujang until well incorporated.

The mayo can be stored in an airtight container in the fridge for up to 2 weeks.

멸치다시마육수

MAKES 1.6–1.9L (7–8 CUPS)

Total time: 30 minutes

1 large brown (yellow) onion, roughly chopped
12 dried shiitake mushrooms
10 myeolchi (large dried anchovies), head and guts removed
6 spring onions (scallions), roughly chopped
8 garlic cloves, crushed
25cm (10in) piece of dashima (dried kelp/kombu)

Anchovy Dashi Stock

Myeolchidasimayuksu

Dashi stock is the chicken broth of Korea. It is the fundamental elixir that is used in so many dishes from kimchi to soups and stews. Nowadays, you can buy sachets full of these dried ingredients and simply drop them into a saucepan like a tea bag. They come in many different flavours, too – dried shrimp, bonito, vegetarian and more. If you can't find dried shiitake mushrooms, you can use dried porcini mushrooms. Note that the guts of the anchovies should be removed as they can make the broth bitter.

In a large saucepan, combine the onion, mushrooms, anchovies, spring onions, garlic and the dashima with 1.9l (8 cups) water, and bring to the boil over a high heat. Reduce the heat and simmer for 20 minutes. Strain the liquid, discarding the solids, and let the stock cool completely.

The stock can be stored in an airtight container in the fridge for up to 1 week or frozen for up to 3 months.

Vegetarian Dashi Stock

Chaesoyuksu

Total time: 30 minutes

1 large brown (yellow) onion, roughly
   chopped
12 dried shiitake mushrooms
6 spring onions (scallions), roughly
   chopped
8 garlic cloves, crushed
25cm (10in) piece of dashima (dried
   kelp/kombu)

This veggie version of dashi stock is still packed full of flavour. Feel free to add another strip of dashima to give this broth a deeper flavour.

In a large saucepan, combine the onion, mushrooms, spring onions, garlic and the dashima with 1.9l (8 cups) water, and bring to the boil over a high heat. Reduce the heat and simmer for 20 minutes. Strain the liquid, discarding the solids, and let the stock cool completely.

The stock can be stored in an airtight container in the fridge for up to 1 week or frozen for up to 3 months

된장쌈장

Doenjang Ssamjang

MAKES 180ML (¾ CUP)

Total time: 5 minutes

5 tbsp doenjang (fermented soya
  bean paste)
1 spring onion (scallion), finely
  chopped
2 tbsp grated brown (yellow) onion
1 tsp grated garlic
1 tbsp mirim
1 tsp caster (superfine) sugar
1 tbsp roasted sesame seeds
2 tsp roasted sesame oil

Ssamjang, or leafy green wrapping sauces, have so many different variations. This one is doenjang-based, sans any spice. I like this one served best with my Perfect Pork Belly Barbecue (see page 96).

Combine all the ingredients in a bowl, place in the fridge and allow the flavours to meld until serving.

The sauce can be stored in an airtight container in the fridge for up to 2 weeks.

쌈장

Ssamjang

MAKES 125ML (½ CUP)

Total time: 5 minutes

2½ tbsp doenjang (fermented soya
  bean paste)
2 tbsp gochujang (Korean chilli paste)
2 tbsp mirim
½ tbsp roasted sesame oil
1 tbsp roasted sesame seeds
1 garlic clove, grated
1 spring onion (scallion), finely
  chopped

Tip
You'll often find samjang served with thin slices of raw garlic with Korean barbecue dishes (see image, page 79).

This is my OG ssamjang recipe that I pretty much slather on everything from barbecue beef to crudités. You can use a spoonful to kick up hummus, chicken soup, or even as a marinade for fish or beef.

In a small bowl, whisk together all the ingredients until smooth. Cover and store in the fridge if not used immediately.

The sauce can be stored in an airtight container in the fridge for up to 2 weeks.

양념장

Jeon Dipping Sauce

Yangnyeomjang

MAKES 80ML (⅓ CUP)

Total time: 5 minutes

60ml (¼ cup) soy sauce
1⅔ tbsp rice vinegar
1 tbsp roasted sesame oil
1 tbsp roasted sesame seeds
2 spring onions (scallions), finely
  chopped, plus 1 tbsp thinly sliced
½ tsp caster (superfine) sugar

This is a classic savoury pancake dipping sauce. Feel free to double this recipe and use it for dumplings (see page 95) and jeon (see pages 40 and 113) alike…even to dress a salad!

Mix together all the ingredients in a bowl and it's ready to serve.

The sauce can be stored in an airtight container in the fridge for up to 2 weeks.

간장양염장

Alternative Jeon Dipping Sauce

Ganjang Yangnyeomjang

MAKES 60ML (¼ CUP)

Total time: 5 minutes

3 tbsp soy sauce
1½ tbsp rice vinegar
3 thin slices of green chilli, preferably
  Korean but a jalapeño will also work
4 thin slices of brown (yellow) onion
3 thin slices of garlic

This is an alternative soy dipping sauce that you'll often see served at Korean restaurants alongside any savoury Korean pancake such as pajeon or bindaetteok (mungbean pancake).

Mix together all the ingredients in a bowl. Serve alongside any savoury pancake of your choice

The sauce can be stored in an airtight container in the fridge for up to 1 week.

Index

Acknowledgements

Thank you so much to my family, my amazing parents, my sister (Sonya), brother-in-law (Kent), little niece (Yuna) and Coco for providing me with unconditional love and support. I love you all so much. I feel so blessed to have such a strong, loving, kind, caring and connected family. Thank you for everything.

And, to my extended family: Helen, Terry, Shinki, Eugene and Jim, Tyler and Caleb (and Kona and Kyra), Eemo and Eemobu, Yuri and Jongmin, Sihun and Seunghee and more ... I feel your love every day even though we live so far apart.

A huge bow of gratitude also to my agent, Martine Carter, and publisher, Jessica Axe, for making this book happen. Thank you also to my co-author and recipe tester and developer, Jessica Do; without your organization, thoughtfulness and talent, I would not have met any of the deadlines. To the best PR team ever, as well – thank you Tara Halper and Jaret Keller for keeping me positive and going the extra mile.

Thank you to the dream production crew: Robert Allison, Emli Bendixen, Alex Breeze and Jessica Do for your talent and vision, and for making my food look so amazing.

Thank you also to Dr Tamar Seckin for performing my life-saving surgery. I would not be the person I am today without your care. I am so grateful for you. And, to Dr Nur Ozyilmaz for helping me tremendously on my road to recovery with so much kindness and wisdom, and for being such a wonderful friend, too.

Thank you to my many dear friends for always being there for me through thick and thin – I would not have gotten this far without you all. You have been my inspiration and my rock.

To my OG girl crew: Jen Kim Chung, Peggy Kauh, Laura Yang, Karen Huh, Susanne Santola Mulligan, Noel Bischoff Sweeny. My dearest and oldest friends, before we had a clue about how tricky and challenging life could be... thank you for seeing me through better and worse, richer and poorer, sickness and health, and more... I love you all so much.

About the Author

Judy Joo is a celebrated Korean-American chef, TV personality and entrepreneur known for her unique blend of Korean and global flavours. Born in New Jersey to Korean immigrant parents, Judy's love for food began at home, where her mother's traditional Korean cooking filled the kitchen with the smells of kimchi, gochujang and drying seaweed. These early influences laid the foundation for her culinary career, which has taken her from Wall Street to world-class kitchens.

After earning an engineering degree from Columbia University, Judy spent several successful years on Wall Street before deciding to follow her true passion: cooking. She enrolled at the French Culinary Institute in New York, where she earned her Grand Diplôme in Pastry Arts. Judy then worked as a test kitchen assistant at *Saveur* magazine before moving to London in 2006 to immerse herself in its vibrant culinary scene. She gained valuable experience as a chef and pastry chef in acclaimed restaurants, including Claridge's, Pétrus and The Boxwood Café, as well as staging at Michelin-starred kitchens like The French Laundry, The Fat Duck and Nahm.

Judy's big break came in 2011 when she became the first female *Iron Chef UK*, a role that launched her into television. She went on to become a regular judge on *Iron Chef America* and a fixture on Food Network. Judy hosted her own shows, *Korean Food Made Simple* and *Judy Joo's Return to Korea*, bringing the rich flavours of Korean cuisine to a global audience. She is the author of *Korean Food Made Simple* and *Korean Soul Food*. *K-Quick: Korean Food in 30 minutes or Less* is her third cookbook.

In 2014, Judy opened her first restaurant, Jinjuu, in London, celebrating modern Korean cuisine. After five years of success, she launched Seoul Bird, a fast-casual concept specializing in Korean fried chicken, with locations in London, Las Vegas and New York. With plans to expand Seoul Bird internationally and new TV projects, Judy's influence on the culinary world continues to go from strength to strength.

Quarto

First published in 2025 by White Lion Publishing
an imprint of The Quarto Group.
One Triptych Place, London, SE1 9SH
United Kingdom
T (0)20 7700 9000
www.Quarto.com

EEA Representation, WTS Tax d.o.o., Žanova ulica 3, 4000 Kranj, Slovenia

A catalogue record for this book is available from the British Library.

ISBN 978-0-7112-9758-6
EBOOK ISBN 978-0-7112-9759-3

10 9 8 7 6 5 4 3 2 1

Book Designer: Claire Rochford
Editorial Director: Jenny Barr
Food Stylist: Rob Allison
Photographer: Emli Bendixen
Photographer's Assistant: Genoveva Arteaga-Rynn
Prop Stylist: Alexander Breeze
Publisher: Jessica Axe
Recipe Tester: Jessica Do
Senior Designer: Renata Latipova
Senior Editor: Charlotte Frost
Senior Production Controller: Rohana Yusof

Printed in China